52 Leadership Stories

Lessons in Talent, Culture and Change

Andy Wild

© Copyright Andy Wild, 2025

The information contained in this book, including, but not limited to text, graphics, images, and other material is protected by copyright.

The author and publisher of this book have made every effort to ensure the accuracy of the information presented; however, they assume no responsibility for errors, omissions, or any consequences arising from the use of the information provided herein.

This book is based on the author's professional experiences, observations, and research. It is intended for informational and educational purposes only. While every effort has been made to ensure accuracy, the author and publisher make no representations or warranties, express or implied, about the completeness, reliability, or applicability of the content

The stories and examples included are for illustrative purposes and may have been adapted or anonymized to respect privacy and confidentiality. Any resemblance to actual persons, living or deceased, or specific organizations is purely coincidental unless explicitly stated.

Reference to ABB, its leaders, or any other organization or individual is solely for context and does not imply endorsement. The views expressed in this book are the author's own and do not reflect those of ABB, its leadership, or any other past or present employer or individual.

This book does not provide legal, financial, or professional advice. Readers are encouraged to apply their own judgment and seek guidance from qualified professionals where necessary. The author and publisher disclaim any liability for actions taken based on the contents of this book.

All rights reserved.

No part of this book may be reproduced or transmitted in any form or by any means, electronic or mechanical including photocopying, recording or by any information storage or retrieval system, without the prior written permission of the copyright owner, except for the use of brief quotations in a book review.

For permissions or inquiries, please contact the author.

ISBN: 978-1-83556-258-1   Paperback
ISBN: 978-1-83556-259-8   Hardback
ISBN: 978-1-83556-260-4   eBook

To Purvashi and April without who's support this book would not have been possible.

To friends and former colleagues who have taught me so much.

Thank you.

CONTENTS

INTRODUCTION — 6

LEADERSHIP — 8

1. Maps, Models, and Frameworks — 10
2. What is Your Model of Leadership? — 12
3. Living at the Apex — 14
4. The Tough Leader Fallacy — 16
5. Every Role Matters — 18
6. Empathy and the JIT Game — 20
7. Being Unreasonable — 22
8. Three Envelopes — 24
9. Cloudline — 26
10. A Skip Full of Wheels — 28
11. Are You OK? — 30
12. Rule No. 6 — 32

CULTURE — 34

13. It's not your culture — 36
14. Pattern Breakers Needed — 38
15. The Lame Duck CEO — 40
16. What your boss pays attention to — 42
17. A Not Taking Ownership Culture — 44
18. When Cultures Meet — 46
19. Discovering Purpose — 48
20. Thinking Systemically — 50
21. Are you an Oyster? — 52
22. My Road to Damascus — 54
23. Getting Customer Focused — 56
24. Nothing is that important — 58

TALENT — 60

25. Building a Talent Mindset — 62
26. The Polarities of Talent Management — 64
27. The Power of Talent Factories — 66

28. Launching Talent Processes _____ 68
29. Managing The Recruitment Factory _____ 70
30. Recruitment Postmortem _____ 72
31. The Barbara Experience _____ 74
32. The 8th Waste _____ 76
33. The Problem With 360 Feedback _____ 78
34. What About 70:20:10? _____ 80
35. The Passion Concept _____ 82
36. How is Your Share Price? _____ 84
37. Everybody's free to wear sunscreen _____ 86

CHANGE _____ 88

38. Can We Change? _____ 90
39. One Firm Spot _____ 92
40. Change Resistance Is Important _____ 94
41. Polarities of Change Communication _____ 96
42. Cascade Meetings For Successful Change _____ 98
43. They left me out of the coffee club _____ 100
44. HRBP Influencing with Impact _____ 102
45. He Bought a Carving Knife _____ 104
46. The Workshop That Never Was _____ 106
47. Over 30 years of Launching Projects _____ 108
48. Bills Form _____ 110
49. The Green Report _____ 112
50. Getting Lunch _____ 114
51. Leading an HR Turnaround _____ 116
52. Dedicated Follower of Fashion _____ 118

WANT TO KNOW MORE _____ 120

ABOUT THE AUTHOR _____ 122

INTRODUCTION

I love ideas.

They have the power to provide fresh perspectives, open doors to new possibilities, unlock intractable problems, and inspire new directions.

Growing up, my mother cooked to the sound of BBC Radio 4. Each morning there was a two-minute segment called "Thought for the Day" . This was a daily reflection on issues and people in the news from a faith-based perspective. I was too young to understand what they were saying, but the idea of a thought for the day stayed with me.

Years later, that early influence resurfaced as I began writing a weekly blog on LinkedIn. Much like 'Thought for the Day,' my blog became a space for sharing reflections, drawing from my thirty-five years of experience in leadership, talent, culture, and transformation. Semi-autobiographical, each post was a snapshot, a thought, or an observation to provoke a moment of reflection. And while the engagement was rewarding, the nature of a LinkedIn post is transitory, a fleeting interaction, like studying a snowflake that melts away a few seconds later and is gone. This book is a collection of fifty-two such stories, edited, updated, and compiled into a more permanent and accessible reference.

The stories are organized into four key themes: Leadership, Culture, Talent and Change, although these topics are very much intertwined. Each story offers a glimpse into the challenges and opportunities I've encountered, lessons learned, and the ideas that emerged along the way. You will see some common themes and ideas that have acted as a foundation for my perspectives. There is the power of questions to

INTRODUCTION

cause a moment of reflection that transforms thinking and action. The importance and awareness of mindsets and mental models behind the actions that we take. There is the fact that much in business is about managing polarities rather than landing on a definitive answer, seeing systems and the human side of change.

Ideas have the power to change the world or at least change our part of the world. To miss quote the British Band Oasis's song lyric, "I started a revolution from my desk, the thoughts I had went to my head."

So here it is. It is not meant to be read in one sitting. It's a resource for reflection, a companion on your own leadership journey. Dip in when you feel the need for inspiration or when a particular challenge arises. It's my hope that these stories will not just spark ideas but also help you shape the kind of leadership that transforms teams, organizations, and individuals for the better.

Andy Wild

Zurich 1st December 2024

Leadership

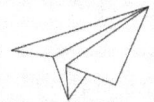

"Great people plant trees whose shade they will never sit under"
Greek Proverb

1 MAPS, MODELS, AND FRAMEWORKS

It was a Tuesday morning, and I found myself sitting in a small conference room with Kevin Martin, Partner of Quarto Consulting; this was the start of my change management skills training, and I was equally excited and mystified about the journey I was beginning. Between us was a brown envelope and a pen. "You are going to learn some effective tools for busy people," explained Kevin, "these are the models you will be able to carry around with you to make sense of complexity, manage relationships, and manage the process of change."

He handed over the envelope; I opened it enthusiastically; inside was a case study of the fictitious company Compile. Kevin left the room, and for the next 60 minutes, I read and re-read the case study and wrote down what I saw as the main business issues and what would be my recommendations. Kevin returned, took my report, and without reading it, sealed it back into the envelope, "We'll look at this again once you have completed the first module of the training and discuss your observations."

This first module was being hosted at the IBM training center; over five days, we were introduced to a powerful toolkit of change models, which we applied in trios to a real business problem we had bought with us. Whether the situation or the person, we learned an integrated toolkit: EDICT, 7P's, Hilltops, 3LT, Pings, BSPI, Culture Triangle, and Cloudline. After five days, I left with a bag of "aha" moments, new tools, new relationships, and a plan to solve my business problem.

Four weeks later, Kevin and I met up in the same conference room, and there between us was that same brown envelope. "Have a look again at the case study, what you wrote and let's discuss what you see," instructed Kevin.

I started reading, and I was shocked, really shocked; this time, I saw underlying issues, unspoken problems, gaps in my understanding, questions that needed to be explored, and much, much more powerful levers for change. Something had happened to me.

Seeing my expression, "You can't influence what you don't understand," Kevin explained, "we have worked hard over the years to make often complex ideas easy to understand. Whether working with individuals or organizations, when attempting to bring about change, it is essential to have a good understanding of with whom and with what you are dealing." "They help you avoid the streetlight effect," said Kevin, "let me explain."

One night, a policeman found a man searching for his keys under a streetlight. He got down on his knees to help; after searching for several minutes, he asked the man, "Are you sure you lost your keys here?" "No, I lost my keys in the park," the man replied. "Then why are you searching here?" asked the policeman. "Because this is where the light is," replied the man.

"These maps, models, and frameworks help us to not just look where the light is," said Kevin, "but to build a more complete understanding. They don't replace our natural curiosity; in fact, our curiosity makes the models even more powerful."

Since then, I have carried these tools with me, going deeper and adding to the toolkit. Kevin's promise never failed to deliver whatever the scenario; I had learned for life a set of tools that helped me understand complexity, manage relationships, and manage change. What tools do you use?

What thinking tools do you use?

2 WHAT IS YOUR MODEL OF LEADERSHIP?

What kind of leader are you, autocratic or democratic? Are you a leader in the mold of Simon Sinek's seal team? Do you create psychological safety or embody a growth mindset? Do you focus on the hard stuff or the soft stuff? Hardheaded or soft-hearted? Are you a servant leader or an entrepreneurial leader?

> *"Only three things happen naturally in organizations: friction, confusion, and underperformance. Everything else requires leadership".*
> **Peter Drucker**

Like many of us, I collect the pithy quotes about leadership, but when it comes to appointing a leader, we need a more robust mental model of leadership.

Business leadership is driving results over the strategic long-term through people (Kelner 2022). Leaders operate in critical situations where their value is put to the test. During my time at ABB, it was important for us to have a clearly defined model of leadership; a global framework, a shared understanding which enabled a consistent style. We considered leadership a combination of behaviors and results, and we built a leadership competency model that balanced business, change, and people. The eight competencies were…

1. Customer focus - Create business value through customers and market understanding
2. Strategic focus - Think beyond the immediate, formulating a plan
3. Results focus – Driving improvement in results, not just achieving goals
4. Change leadership - Transform and align an organization to a new direction

5. Team leadership - The ability to focus, align, and build effective groups
6. People development - Developing the long-term capabilities of others and the organization
7. Collaboration - Working with others who are not in the line of their command
8. Diversity and inclusiveness - Ability to embrace and leverage different perspectives

Eight might seem too many; after all, "simple is best." Like Microsoft's leadership values, create clarity, generate energy, and deliver success. This apparent simplicity is appealing and helpful when it comes to communication, but under the hood, you realize the complexity remains.

We found our leaders adopted the eight competencies and we developed a process for leaders to reflect on their leadership performance using them. We ran the development assessment for more than 10 years and amassed an extensive data set. Our analysis revealed how the process had positively impacted the career development of our leaders and the strength of our leadership bench.

- What is your mental model of leadership?
- How many of the eight competencies does it cover?
- How do you measure up?

3 LIVING AT THE APEX

In 2002 Google tried to prove managers weren't needed. They didn't succeed. Instead, it became clear without a manager, employees felt lost and left without direction and guidance. Called Project Oxygen, they switched focus onto the opposite question, "What are the common behaviors of the very best managers?"

Gallup's research identified that 70% of engagement is down to the manager, echoing a study conducted by McBer & Company that showed between 50-70% of the work environment is created by the leadership style of the direct manager. More than anyone else, the manager creates the conditions that directly determine people's ability to work well.

In 2014, Zurich Insurance conducted a study into their leaders, discovering that 70% would not choose to be people managers again. These results are not isolated to one company.

First-line managers are at the apex of many topics and challenges. The transition to people manager could be the most important career transition of all. Although often a very junior appointment, not given much focus however, the impact of getting it wrong can last a career, reverberating out into the organisation through the teams they manage.

Talent management is about movement and ensuring we make high-quality people decisions. We should not promote people because they perform well or because we like them but because we see their potential to lead others.

To address this issue, in ABB we launched a first-line manager assessment center for individual contributors who wanted to become people managers. During the launch of the first assessments, we found that around 30% of those nominated were simply not suitable; in fact, many were not actually interested but were either pushed by their manager to attend or saw no other opportunity for a promotion.

Healthy organisations need healthy managers comfortable with the role they have been assigned. Willing and able. Clayton M. Christensen. Harvard Business School Professor described management.

> *"In my mind's eye, I saw one of my managers leave home for work one morning with a relatively strong level of self-esteem. Then I pictured her driving home to her family 10 hours later, feeling unappreciated, frustrated, underutilized, and demeaned. I imagined how profoundly her lowered self-esteem affected the way she interacted with her children. The vision in my mind then fast-forwarded to another day when she drove home with greater self-esteem – feeling that she had learned a lot, been recognized for achieving valuable things, and played a significant role in the success of some important initiatives. I then imagined how positively that affected her as a spouse and as a parent."*

Management is the most noble of professions if it's practiced well. No other occupation offers as many ways to help others learn and grow, take responsibility, be recognized for achievement, and contribute to the success of a team.

Managers are living at the apex.

4   THE TOUGH LEADER FALLACY

I was told to leave the leader well alone. His Region was delivering results, no need to interfere. I wondered, were my beliefs about leadership, right? Maybe the tough manager was the better model?

When, finally, the business struggled, I was asked to help. What I found under the hood was not strength and competence but nasty internal conflict, high turnover, upset customers, and missed opportunities. The apparent "good" performance had only been a fraction of what was possible. Rather than delivering results, the tough leader had held back what good leadership could have enabled. Lesson learned.

Dr James McQuivey of Forrester Research highlighted the fallacy of the tough leadership model…

> *"Unflinching leaders like George Patton and Douglas Macarthur could accomplish things other leaders cannot, or so the story goes. The idea that tough leaders always win is a fallacy; the equally tough leaders on the German and Japanese sides did not win. For every successful explosive entrepreneur, there will be a myriad of pound-shop wannabes acting like jerks. For every Jerk that succeeds, there are thousands that fail dismally."*

The tough leader is too often scoring own goals, breeding fear, with team members who avoid risk-taking and the potential consequences. Human-centered leadership is a recent trend, triggered in part by the pandemic. I appreciate the focus on topics like psychological safety or growth mindset; however, they only tell half the story; we don't just need the secure base but also the stretch and challenge.

George Kohlrieser in his book Care to Dare, highlights the need to balance the kindness (care) that provides the secure base for work with the toughness (dare) that provides the challenge and stretch to achieve more. How might leaders do this?

LEADERSHIP

I was due to present my strategy to the CEO, but I was never sure how these meetings would go. On arrival I found a CEO relaxed and patient. We sat at his meeting table, laptops off; he wanted to hear my thoughts unfiltered by PowerPoint, to listen and discuss. I felt the confidence to be more forthright and bold as I shared my observations and proposed plan. He was engaged. Then something remarkable happened.

"This proposal has everything we need," he said, "but Andy, I can imagine from your previous experience you need to go forward carefully, but we don't have time. The market is growing fast, and we need to move fast. I have a challenge for you. How can we engage everyone so they know something has changed in the first year, not three years?"

I was astonished; I am used to being slowed down, not sped up. I left his office vibrating; I needed to dig deep, go beyond the obvious, and find an approach to create a step change, not an incremental one.

- What kind of leader are you?
- A tough leader or a human-centered leader?
- Or better still, can you balance the care and the dare?

5 EVERY ROLE MATTERS

We were leaderless; our Division Manager had left.

The search for his replacement was progressing but was not close to being concluded, so the CEO stepped in ad interim. He called us together for our first leadership meeting. We all knew him but every manager has their own way of running things, we were curious to see what changes he would bring. However, this first meeting was a sobering experience.

The CEO wanted to get an update on what everyone was doing and agree on what our priorities would be going forward. However, as we went through the agenda, he continually challenged us, "HR, have you involved the business in this?" "Business Manager, have you involved HR in this?". Each time, he was clear: were the team working together, were the right people involved? Was every role contributing to the business as they should?

We left the meeting a little dazed. Over the two hours we all felt like we had had our heads knocked together. While not fun then, it created a mindset shift and a behavior change. Each of the roles needed to play their part.

Over the years, I have seen leaders who don't fully take some roles in their team seriously; they sometimes include them, sometimes not. They don't fully believe in the importance of the role to the leadership team, almost humoring them to be politically correct.

Steven Drotter & Ram Charan, in their book The Leadership Pipeline, published in 2000, highlighted the transitions leaders make as they progress through the different stages of their leadership careers.

- From Individual Contributor to Leading Others
- From Leading Others to Leading Leaders
- From Leading Leaders to Functional Leaders
- From Functional Leader to Business Leader

At each transition point or "turn", a change in mindset needs to happen. This mindset change indicates whether the leader has really stepped up into their new role or whether they are still trying to lead as if it were their previous role, the sales manager managing their business as if it's a sales team first.

A key function of leadership is to build and align effective teams, getting each role to play its part and working together for the overall mission.

- How do you view each role in your team?
- Do you have favorites or roles you see as less important?
- How do you ensure each function plays its role?

6   EMPATHY AND THE JIT GAME

We were implementing lean manufacturing, and to build understanding and support, we ran a lean manufacturing game for everyone in the factory. They came in groups of 12-18 for a presentation, the JIT Game, conclusions, and discussion. The sessions were lively, with plenty of pushback and challenging questions; it was healthy engagement.

The goal had been to cover everyone. However, each time one of the shop floor team members was scheduled to come, they didn't show up. After the third time this happened, we clearly had a problem. I was a somewhat ambitious and zealous young change manager and wanted this resistor to be dealt with. The supervisor was a bit perplexed but also concerned, so he called the production worker to his office for a meeting to find out what was going on. It was clear to me the employee was in trouble.

I caught up with the supervisor later in the day to find out what happened.

"It was a difficult meeting", he explained.

Oh no, I thought, "in what way?"

"It turns out he was afraid to come."

"Really?" I said, "but why?"

"I discovered the reason was he can hardly read and write. He had hidden this from everyone for years. He was afraid during the session he would need to read or write and would finally be exposed."

"Oh no, what did you do?" I asked

"Of course, I was astonished he had been able to hide it," said the supervisor. "he admitted he had developed many strategies to keep it hidden. He would say he forgot his glasses, be too busy, ask someone to read for him, have dirty hands or pretend to have a hand injury to not write."

"But why?" I asked.

"He thought once he was exposed, he would lose his job. Actually, he's a great worker, productive, consistent, and good-spirited. I cannot imagine losing him. So, I told him he should have come to me before, we will sponsor evening classes for him as part of our continuous learning policy. He was quite emotional and very grateful."

"Andy, I have been a supervisor for 25 years. You touch the tip of the iceberg of people's lives, even the ones you get really close to, but there is so much you don't know. I have learned the wise seek to understand first before acting."

I learned a lesson that day.

The production worker finally joined the next session. Knowing who he was, I gave him the starring role in the JIT Game, the one with the electric screwdriver who does the final assembly.

He enjoyed the session with some pride as he had overcome something that had been a shadow over him for many years.

7   BEING UNREASONABLE

"To achieve great things, two things are needed:
a plan and not quite enough time."
Leonard Bernstein

The business was falling short of its targets; everyone had already been squeezed, but we needed another round of action.

During the Local Business Unit reviews, John, the BU Manager, laid out the case for change and what was required. Understandably, there was a lot of pushback; each local business complained there was nothing left to give.

I was surprised; I always viewed John as smart and rational. It seemed to me that setting this kind of challenge flew in the face of logic. After the calls, I asked him, "Do you really think it's reasonable to ask them to find more? After all the cost reductions, do they really have more to give?"

"No, it's not reasonable," he replied, "and I don't know what they can achieve. But I have set them the challenge now; let's see what they come back with."

"But aren't you just frustrating everyone?" I inquired.

"Whatever they say on the calls, I know they trust me, and they understand that if I'm asking, it's for a good reason—it's important. They can see I'm under pressure, which signals that the global business is under pressure too."

A week later, I sat with John for an update.

LEADERSHIP

"Well, it turns out some of the Local Units still had something to give; clearly, they had kept some back for a "rainy day", now they let it go because the rainy day had come."

"Some units could do nothing; they were already squeezed dry. I could forgive them that."

"For others, they had something to give because the challenge meant they needed to dig deep, push harder, get creative, or maybe they simply got lucky with a customer order coming early."

"Overall, we made it. I am proud of what they have achieved and I know they also feel the satisfaction of being able to deliver."

While we talk about human-centered leadership, this does not preclude us from setting challenges and expecting our teams to stretch for goals that seem a little out of reach. Psychological safety is not about being soft but rather about providing the climate for speaking up and challenging for better solutions and greater results.

My BU Manager could push because he understood the need for care and dare. Care, the climate for openness, honesty, risk-taking, and the dare, the stretch, challenge, and ambition for something more.

- How are you creating psychological safety?
- How well do you create challenge and stretch?
- How well are you balancing them?

8 THREE ENVELOPES

This story is based on real events; the names have been changed to protect the innocent, but the facts remain the same.

A new CEO was hired to take over a struggling company. The CEO stepping down was clearing his desk when the new CEO arrived. Welcoming him, the exiting CEO offered some advice.

"I know the CEO's job is tough; if you ever get stuck, I have left three envelopes in the top drawer of your desk. Each one contains some practical advice," he said.

The new CEO thanked him but also inside scoffed at such a suggestion. He was confident he would transform this struggling business.

Some months later, things were not going well, and the new CEO was under tremendous pressure. He remembered the three envelopes. Going back to his desk drawer, he took out the first envelope and opened it. The message read,

"Blame your predecessor."

Of course, he thought. The new CEO called a press conference and explained that the previous CEO had left him with a much more serious mess than was first known, and it would take longer to turn around the business. Satisfied with his announcement, the press and Wall Street responded positively.

But another few quarters went by, and the company continued to struggle. Having learned from his previous experience, the CEO quickly opened the second envelope, curious to see the advice. The message read,

"Announce a reorganization."

"Yes, of course," he thought, "we need a better structure". So, he changed the structure, consolidated divisions, and cut costs everywhere he could. Wall Street and the press applauded his efforts.

But as the quarters passed the company was still in trouble. Sitting at his desk, the CEO, struggling with what to do, remembered the last envelope. He reached into the draw and took out the last envelope. Carefully, he opened it and read the simple message inside…

"Write three envelopes."

The story tickled me the first time I heard it; it still does now. There is something in the story that chimes with our experiences.

Business is full of repeating patterns. We need to notice them. A new manager often brings a new structure, but business is more than structure. We should look deeper into the system and mental models behind the patterns for transformation to truly happen.

9 CLOUDLINE

In the company there had been a culture of telling their bosses what they wanted to hear.

Project problems were not reported in the hope they could be fixed later, the company fell into crisis and the Board exited the CEO.

When the new CEO joined the project managers were taken by surprise, his questions showed he knew their projects, even to issues they were not yet aware. How was this possible?

The new CEO had learned how to stay grounded. His habit was to walk the shop floor at 7.30 in the morning and talk to the assemblers, welders, and logistics. At first, no one knew who he was; over time, he became a familiar face, but it seemed to not affect the employee's willingness to tell it as it is. Why? Because he always showed genuine interest in learning and understanding. By the time he sat in the monthly project reviews, he was well informed; they became transparent and constructive meetings. He transformed the culture.

It is easy for a CEO to become isolated, called the Cloudline effect. At the top of the mountain, it's a clear blue sky; you can see for miles. Looking down, the clouds obscure the foot of the mountain; it's difficult to know what is going on down there without descending.

This is more than a skip level meeting and is a common strategy of successful leaders I have worked with. They build networks of people, they visit, take unannounced walks and keep in touch with the pulse of the company. This is not driven by a lack of trust but a necessity to stay grounded.

We can all benefit from this as leaders. I took these lessons to my global roles; I found trusted partners in the organization that kept me in touch with reality, and as uncomfortable as it was sometimes, it made me more effective.

But is it possible to replicate some of this effect in the virtual and hybrid world? When the pandemic prevented normal coffee machine discussions, the CEO of Stanley, the water bottle company, decided each Friday he would call random employees on Zoom. It became known as the President Flybys.

The secret is not just doing it but how you do it. As a senior leader, your power can silence the truth, and we may act in ways that discourage our employees. How is your listening face? Does it encourage employees to share issues and problems? This has been well covered in the book "Speak Up: Say What Needs to Be Said and Hear What Needs to Be Heard" by Megan Reitz and John Higgins.

What can we take away….

- Find people who are not in your world of above-the-clouds
- Find people who are willing to not just tell you what you want to hear
- Be aware of your listening face, the body language signals you send when listening
- Be aware and moderate your response if you want to be told again
- Be curious to understand their perspective; climb down from your Hilltop to see the world from theirs
- Act on what you learn
- You might be surprised by what you find below the clouds.

10 A SKIP FULL OF WHEELS

> *"I've seen things you people wouldn't believe... Attack ships on fire off the shoulder of Orion... I watched C-beams glitter in the dark near the Tannhäuser Gate. All those moments will be lost in time, like tears in rain... Time to die."*
> **Roy Batty, Bladerunner**

As we reorganized the business, desks were moved, cupboards emptied, and databases archived. Looking through all this stuff, I was amazed to see all the projects that had been completed, what must be millions and millions of dollars spent on consultancies, studies, and project work that ended up in abandoned cupboards and now destined to be thrown in the skip. All this knowledge and tools built up would now be disposed of and lost to time. I decided they should find a home and offered them to colleagues but was flatly told, "Nobody wants this old stuff."

In business we often talk about the idea of reinventing the wheel. Unnecessarily developing a new solution when one already exists. I looked at the large bin with all the folders and documents to be securely disposed of. It was like looking at a bin full of wheels that had been invented, and now nobody feels responsible for it. In fact, in the desire to march forward the old is discarded only to be reinvented years later.

I think this reflects the difficulty of organizational learning; we keep paying for new wheels. After 35 years, the company could be the world's expert on many topics if it could capture all that knowledge, insight, and learning. It could write a book on so many topics.

It's exciting to see how AI is changing how we interact with information, the ability to access knowledge in such a way that it goes beyond regurgitated lists and synthesizes it into something more useful.

But having access to the information is not enough; without the curiosity to ask and the humility to learn, it may as well have been destined to the bin.

Italian philosopher Antonio Gramsci once stated that history is a great teacher but does not have many students.

La Storia insegna ma non ha Scolari

History teaches but has no Scholars

When you look out the back of your offices, what do you see, a skip full of wheels?

11   ARE YOU OK?

I always wondered where the term OK came from.

I finally discovered the following story during a Lean Manufacturing training program.

> *"In 1929, in the Ford River Rogue Plant, there was a Quality Manager responsible for inspecting every Model T Ford that left the end of the line. As he inspected the car, he put his initials against each inspection item. The Quality Inspectors name was Oscar Krauss, and so O.K. became a term for something being right, to standard, or acceptable."*

Sadly, as much as I love the story, it's not true, and repeating it here doesn't make it any more true. OK's origins are disputed; however, most modern reference works hold that it originated around Boston as part of a fad for misspelling in the late 1830s, and originally stood for "oll korrect" (Ref Wikipedia). This clearly pre-dates the Ford story.

So, what does it mean to be OK?

Eric Berne, the father of Transactional Analysis, defined OK-ness as the most fundamental assumption about people. He believes that we all have inherent value and are worthy of being treated with dignity and respect regardless of behavior or life circumstances.

People are OK: Ok-ness is not earned.

In our world of work, "OK-ness" is important: a belief that "I'm OK, you're OK". It powers psychological safety, how we work together effectively, and our impact on others.

Some days, we don't feel it, but it doesn't change the fact.

I'm OK and so are you, let's get to work!

12

RULE NO. 6

I was stressed.

Integrating the new acquisition was not easy; it was like riding a wild Tiger. The company had invested $1bn, a large amount of money, which was at risk because of the people issues. As the HR responsible I had a lot to contend with.

I found myself in the CHRO's office, reporting on how it was going. I was speaking fast, trying to download what I had discovered and what we were doing about it.

Gary, the CHRO, sat calmly listening.

Then he put his hand on my shoulder and said, "Andy, don't forget rule number 6."

I looked at him blankly.

"Rule number 6? What's that?"

"Don't take yourself so damn seriously," replied Gary

I smiled as I felt a weight come off my shoulders. I left his office no less determined but with a better sense of perspective.

As I reached the door, I had one final question.

"Gary, what are the other 5 rules?"

"After rule number 6," replied Gary

"There are no other rules."

I think there are two takeaways here. We may think what we do is vital but we are mostly not curing cancer or preventing nuclear war, keep a realistic perspective. Secondly, we play an important role as leaders to provide our team members with a healthy sense of perspective.

Next time you find yourself in this kind of situation, remember...

Rule No.6

Rule No.6 was inspired by a story shared in chapter 6 of the book The Art of Possibility: Transforming Professional and Personal Life by Rosamund Stone Zander and Benjamin Zander.

Culture

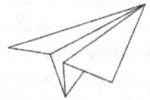

"We shape our buildings, and afterwards our buildings shape us."
Winston Churchill

13   IT'S NOT YOUR CULTURE

> *"Hardly any term is thrown about more carelessly and with less accuracy than organizational culture."*

Culture is often taking the credit or blame for what goes on in companies, it seems to me to be doing a lot of heavy lifting. Culture is not easily seen, like asking a fish about the water they swim in. It surfaces in the patterns of the organization, "the way we do things around here"; however, it is the underpinning assumptions and mental models that drive the culture.

Participating in a culture simulation exercise some years back, I was confronted by both the speed and power of culture. The exercise split the group into two, the "Talls" and the "Shorts", the Talls followed a set of individualistic behaviors with no physical contact, and the Shorts followed a collective, high physical touch set of behaviors. After some minutes, the two groups were asked to work together on a common task. I was shocked; there was an immediate and powerful clash of cultures. It had taken only a few minutes for each of the two groups to so identify with their group's behaviors for them to become resilient to change. This clash of cultures deeply impacted the two groups' ability and productivity to work together. The different cultures became an obstruction to collaboration.

Walking back through my cultural transformation experiences, my success came from changing the day-to-day experiences employees had. We act our way into a new culture, not communicate our way there. Breaking old patterns and establishing new ones. In Daniel Goldman's book Primal Leadership he references a study that identified 50-70% of the work environment is created by the leadership style of the direct manager. If culture eats strategy for breakfast, then leadership eats culture for breakfast. If culture is to change, then mobilizing leadership is a key step and an important starting point.

Leaders can do five things to shape culture...

- Model the culture - Act your way there, map the culture to your daily responsibilities, and re-balance the time you spend to reflect the new culture more closely.
- Involve others to live the culture - transfer the ownership, collaborate on what needs to change and how
- Help others break from the past culture - call out old behaviors, support their efforts, challenge their assumptions, and think through pattern-breaking incidents.
- Create a supportive learning environment - we are always practicing not getting it right, no blame or know-it-alls, and provide maps and models that codify the culture and behaviors.
- Communicate the culture - a following activity, not a leading activity; communication still plays a role in making the culture more conscious and visible.

Building a thriving culture starts with action, focusing less on communication and more on closing the gap between what you say and what you do. Culture in the halls vs culture on the walls. Not a statement on a poster but in the hearts of the people.

Edger Schien reminds us that culture change should be purposeful, something that is needed to operate more effectively in the market. It should solve a problem and not be an end unto itself, to manifest behaviors that will enable the business to be more competitive and successful.

If you can't see it, then it's not your culture.

14 PATTERN BREAKERS NEEDED

As the crisis intensified, Jürgen Dormann, the Chairman, stepped in as CEO of ABB.

His first executive team meeting was in Sweden, with the team needing to fly in from Switzerland. As the rest of the executives sat on the plane in Business Class, they saw the new CEO join the flight at the last minute, walk past them, and sit in the economy at the back of the plane. Upon arrival in Sweden the other executives rushed to their limo's while Mr Dormann quietly walked to the bus stop. Without comment or fanfare, he sent a powerful message to the leadership team that a new way of behaving was expected. On the return trip, he was no longer alone in economy.

There was no communication launch; this was not a publicity stunt but a reflection of an authentic pattern-breaking leader. Without waiting for the results of a cultural diagnosis, without announcing a plan, he "lived the future now". It was a story that permeated into the cultural fabric of ABB.

This was not an isolated instance nor isolated to Jürgen Dormann. A very vocal and cynical colleague of mine had commented on an intranet article posted by Gary Steel, the new Global Head of HR. One Friday morning, out of the blue, my colleague received a phone call from Gary. I watched as he discussed and debated openly and directly with him; he left the phone call a changed man. Before, the leadership had seemed very far away and remote from our business life; in a moment, the many layers of the hierarchy had been compressed. This single phone call resonated for months after and was an often-told story years later. It had a disproportionate impact to the few minutes invested.

CULTURE

Senior leaders have a powerful pattern-breaking role, signalling something is different, not by words but by action. Despite what might be expected, Jürgen Dormann was not a larger-than-life character, but you might say modest and low-key leader. However, he was authentic; he brought clarity, and his actions spoke for him. Culture change happens because we change the day-to-day working experiences employees have. Too many culture changes lead with communication, but communication is a vehicle to share those experiences, like with Jürgen, who started a weekly letter to all employees to do just that.

Gandhi said, "Be the change you wish to see". The more senior the leader, the more significant impact they have in changing employees' day-to-day experiences.

Be a pattern breaker, be authentic, and live the patterns that will energize the new culture.

15 THE LAME DUCK CEO

The CEO had left, so Peter, the Chairman, took the helm of the business. He quickly got to work, reaffirming the strategy and laying out the top five priorities. Alongside traveling extensively and holding town hall meetings, Peter held the company's first global virtual town hall. A one-and-a-half-hour video call dedicated to answering employee's questions posted live on Yammer.

I was sitting in a large conference room in HQ watching the call, and about halfway through, the Head of Communications read out this question.

"Don't you think, as a lame duck CEO, we are going to lose time waiting for the new CEO."

In the room there was an audible intake of breath, then an embarrassed laugh. This kind of question was shocking. Silently, we listened to see how Peter would respond. Calmly, he explained, there is only ever one CEO at a time and while it was him, he would act and take decisions as if he were the permanent CEO.

Two weeks later, I sat with Peter at breakfast when he joined us during our HR Leadership Team Workshop, and we discussed the incident.

"That was quite some question you were asked during the virtual Townhall," I said.

"I took the question deliberately," Peter answered. "You see, as a leader, you need to show what kind of culture you expect, and I mean show. We don't need to make big announcements that the culture is changing; we just need to start doing it."

"But the question was, you could say, quite rude" I added.

"While the question was clumsy" replied Peter "However, I saw there was a genuine underlying concern I felt needed to be addressed, and in answering such a question, it provided me with an opportunity to role model my expectations of our leaders"

Over the nine months Peter was interim CEO he could be found walking the offices, hands in pockets, chatting to people. His early and intense travel schedule involved meeting and speaking to as many employees as possible. He truly got a sense of the mind and pulse of the company, as did they of him.

Peter was no less focused on performance, the momentum was maintained, a new company purpose was defined, an engagement survey was launched, and a refocusing on sustainability. But at the same time, he was approachable, accessible, and transparent, bringing the people with him.

We act our way into a new culture, not communicate our way there.

16   WHAT YOUR BOSS PAYS ATTENTION TO

As leaders, we can forget the unintended influence we have.

While running a "Leading a Healthy and Safe Culture" course, we gave each leadership team an assignment to go out into the factory and conduct a simple safety audit.

The CEO was rarely seen in the factory, so his presence was well noted. As required by the instructions we had given him, he went up to an assembly team to ask what procedures they should follow and what personal protective equipment (PPE) they should wear. As he was requested to do, the CEO listened, issued no instruction, and wrote down the answers on the audit sheet. After he left, the supervisor ran over to the team in panic to find out what the CEO had asked. Within 30 minutes of the CEO leaving, the team was fitted out and wearing their new PPE.

Paul Anderson, then CEO of BHP Billiton, the Australian mining and metals company, had a similar experience. He was driving a turnaround of the business and one of the key issues was safety. After a strong safety campaign, he was not satisfied with the results and called the Head of Health & Safety to his office.

"How come the organization isn't embracing a safety culture?" He asked.

The H&S Manager paused, weighing up how he should say it. Finally, he replied, "Well, you're the problem."

"What!" responded Anderson. "I couldn't be more committed to safety"

CULTURE

"Well, the problem is you're a lousy role model. People notice you don't hold the handrail when you walk up and down stairs, you don't park backward into a parking space, your first question to managers is about financial performance, at the weekend employees see how you work on your house and garden."

Paul Anderson was stunned; he learned an important lesson that day as a leader. People judge your commitment not by what you say but by your actions. "Your actions are too loud; I can't hear what you are saying." Parents know this all too well.

Like it or not as a leader, we are being watched. Employee behavior can be shaped by what we pay attention to, whether positive or negative.

Leaders can eat culture for breakfast or cook a new one.

It can be trite to say we need to "walk the talk". Maybe we should "talk what we walk".

What would your teams conclude from your behavior?

17 A NOT TAKING OWNERSHIP CULTURE

We met over a coffee, keen to catch up. My friend showed me the culture change initiative he had just taken over for his business. The theme "taking ownership" was a positive one, an ambition of a large business to empower all its employees.

"So, what do you think?" my friend asked.

"Wow, it's an impressive deck" I replied. "I can clearly see the amount of work that has gone into it"

"Come on, Andy, what do you really think?"

"Yea ok, what troubles me about this initiative" I responded "is it looks like a communication exercise, for example living the values is step three. It's advocating and imploring employees to take ownership, but what is changing to make this a reality? It seems the assumption is that employees don't take ownership because no one has told them to."

My friend was silent. Then he said.

"We are nine months in, and I have been asked to present some success stories. I have them but the problem is they all predate the initiative. What should we do?"

""It's good to start by building on what you have learnt so far. However, I have come to the conclusion based on hard-bitten experience that we act our way into a new culture, not communicate our way there. Culture happens when we change the experience employees have in their day-to-day work. It's interesting; we blame the culture but target the individual."

"What do you mean?" he probed.

"When the flower doesn't bloom, you fix the environment, not the flower. If culture is more than the individual, we need to examine how the structures, systems, and mental models help or hinder an ownership-taking culture. One of the structures is the leaders; they have the greatest influence on culture."

"For example, managers refusing to decide something and instead asking their teams and team members to decide. Changing the approval levels in the systems. Calling out non-ownership behaviors in real-time and employees feeling the discomfort. Creating clearer accountability to reduce the possibility of blaming someone else. Managers taking ownership themselves as a role model, stopping their own blame behaviors."

"OK, I get your point." my friend paused for a moment. "When I think about it, probably the initiative should have been called….."

"….give ownership, not take ownership!"

"Shifting and managing a culture is not about telling people what to do and expecting them to neatly fall in line, but about recognizing where they really are and how they make decisions so that you can start to shift the environment, influencing them to make different decisions and form new habits."

18 WHEN CULTURES MEET

Culture is something we all participate in, whether it is the country we live in, the company we work at, our local sports club, or our family. Groups always create their own unique culture, and that's fine, as culture is something we unconsciously create for the success and survival of the group. It binds us together.

We don't think of our culture as strange; in fact, it's so familiar to us that we become blind to it, and it becomes just the way things are. Only when we encounter a different culture do we become aware there are other ways to do things other than our own?

Many of us went through this the first time we went abroad on our annual summer holiday. The way "they" queue or not, put "their" towels on the sunbeds or tip the waiter. How do we react? "Isn't it strange?" Often, we are glad to return home for some real home cooking. Aah, back to civilization.

So, when cultures meet, our response can sometimes be like the archetypal colonialist; we act like a dominant nation to civilize the world. They must fit in with our ways.

In our business life, cultures meet constantly; we integrate an acquisition, merge two businesses or two departments or two functions, and multiple companies work in partnership to deliver a large project. The dynamics are the same, "isn't it strange how they...." we act dominant, and the merging of cultures just doesn't go well; it's an unsettling process for everyone.

There is a massive amount written about defining and codifying culture. However, what is absent from what is published about culture is what happens when we bring two cultures together? I've had a series of personal experiences of being acquired and merged. I've managed integrations and mergers, and despite many good "team building" activities, it still left a series of unresolved frustrations. Why was this? What was missing?

What I discovered through working with Barry Oshry were ways of understanding the dynamics of when cultures meet. Barry is one of the worlds leading thinkers on human systems and organizations, who has worked with hundreds of world-class organizations over the last fifty years. He highlights the dynamics of "Dominant" and "Other" and our tendency to Preserve/Protect our own culture. There is almost an unsaid assumption in a merger, "we are driving for one culture to be adopted, the Dominant's culture". Does this mean we really want everyone to be the same (which is a drive for "homogenization")? It's easily done without conscious thought, however, the consequences of which would be to drive out the strengths of the "Others" and only allow for the strengths we already have. It's not a recipe for reaping the value of bringing two groups together. The reverse equally doesn't work to preserve differentiation of the "Others" or, in the extreme, to allow them to be dominant.

The solution is not to diminish differentiation but to put equal and opposite energy into both homogenization (identifying and developing our commonalities, working on our sameness) and differentiation (giving space for our differences).

As leaders in our merger situations our challenge is to be aware of these issues and make helpful choices that will lead to positive outcomes. Next time we bring two groups together, ask ourselves:-

- Do we seek to create a partnership between the two that creates something greater from the diversity?
- Who is Dominant? Who is Other? And what are the results we are seeing?
- What is happening to drive for both homogenization and differentiation?

19 DISCOVERING PURPOSE

Empires do not suffer an emptiness of purpose at the time of their creation. It is when they have become established that aims are lost and replaced by vague ritual.
Taken from Dune by Frank Herbert

Purpose statements have become fashionable in recent years, although the best business leaders have always understood their power. A sense of purpose answers the question of Why. Simon Sinek may be best known for his TED Talk on the concept of Why, which has been viewed over 60 million times. For companies, it is the reason for being beyond what it does, make, or sell.

Satya Nardella reflected on the progress he made with Microsoft, "When I look back, I didn't know this as clearly then, but perhaps the most useful thing I've done is to anchor us in a sense of purpose, mission, and identity". Satya observed he was not an original Microsofter, he was not there for its founding, he realized he needed to become a refounder. Refind that DNA and sense of purpose.

A McKinsey survey from 2020 showed that 85% of executives believe they are living their company's purpose. However, 85% of front-line workers are unsure or disagree. As the saying goes, how to "get it off the walls and into the halls".

A meaningful purpose should guide everything, not just a slogan without teeth. Something that reaches people at an emotional level, gets under their skin if you like.

It had been many weeks of Steve Jobs courting John Sculley, then PepsiCo president, for the role of CEO of Apple. Finally, John let Steve know he had decided not to join. Disappointed, Steve left John with a challenge that would go on to haunt him, "Do you want to spend the rest of your life selling sugared water, or do you want to

CULTURE

change the world?" Sculley said the question landed like "a punch to the gut." it questioned his sense of purpose.

Time and time again I have discovered the power of purpose is massively underestimated. In ABB we returned to the question of purpose, rediscovering it as we transformed the group through the ABB Way. As I have worked through integrating many acquisitions, I have discovered it is not just the company purpose but how we enable employees to discover their own purpose and connection to the organization as things change. I love the 7P's analytical framework, developed by Quarto Consulting, as a systemic and practical tool for anchoring purpose at the center of any transformation.

As you jump out of bed in the morning, for you and your colleagues, how is your sense of purpose or have you fallen into a vague ritual?

20 THINKING SYSTEMICALLY

He was late back from the coffee break, and it was disrupting the training. On the flip chart was the systems iceberg (events, patterns, systemic structures, mental models). Originally developed by Chris Argyris and Donald Schon and later described in Peter Senge's The Fifth Discipline (1990).

"To recap," I said, "we often see events, stuff happens, we solve it, but it happens again, it becomes a pattern of events", pointing to the flip chart, "Patterns are a window into seeing the system behind it".

"Let me give you an example: John came in late to this session. That's an event. But, you probably haven't noticed, John has been late back to all the sessions. A pattern of events". The group nodded in recognition.

John spoke up. "Sorry, everyone, but I really have too much work, and there is only me in the office; I am trying to keep the work going so I can attend the course."

"OK, but let's look at what structures we could work on to solve this," I proposed. "OK" said John

"Well, maybe you just put an out-of-office instead so people know the answer will be delayed," "Not possible," he replied, "I am answering technical queries, and they cannot wait; we have a metric for that." "How about a database of FAQs?" "Not possible; the technical questions are too complex and varied, and anyway, they expect to speak to a person"

Each time I suggested a solution, he had a reason it would not work. Another pattern.

"Hang on a minute," I turned to the flip chart with the iceberg drawn on it.

"We have worked through the event, the patterns of events, gone below the water line to the systemic structures. But every solution proposed you have rejected. When we get stuck like this, we should explore the mental models driving the structures and pattern of events." Pointing to the deepest point at the bottom of the flip.

I turned to John. "Let's explore your mental model. What is it about your way of thinking that allows this condition to persist?" I could see John thinking hard, seriously considering the question, then his face broke into a smile.

"To be honest, Andy, I like being indispensable; it gives me a sense of importance and reinforces my expertise!"

Systems thinking is a discipline for seeing problems holistically and for understanding how systems create the patterns and events we see around us. We live in an event-driven world; it is easier to notice events than patterns and systemic structures. To become a systems thinker, we need to start by developing our own awareness and skills. Often, we need to extend our time horizon and look at the bigger picture.

To be a good systems thinker, use these four questions...

1. What just happened?
2. Have we been here before?
3. What are the forces at play?
4. What is it about our way of thinking that allows this condition to persist?

How is your systems thinking?

21

ARE YOU AN OYSTER?

It was day two of the personal leadership program and we were debriefing the participants self-assessments of how they interacted with their colleagues. How much did they share information, and how much they inquired?

Everyone's results were different; however, there were some predictable patterns. Some talked more, some inquired more, some did both, and some did neither. We gave each style a nickname: Lecturer, Interviewer, Full Engagement, and Oyster.

Some participants were very uncomfortable with what this self-reflection revealed about their communication patterns. It seemed they wanted to explain it away, and almost without fail, the comment would come…

"If you knew my boss, then you also would act like this"

What were they really saying?

"My behavior is not my fault; it's someone else's"

Each time this happened with a group, it allowed me to go deeper into personal leadership, reflect on the mental model I was hearing, and increase their self-awareness.

"So you are saying your boss controls your behavior, not you."

"Well, err…." The cogs would start spinning.

"Are you saying you are not able to choose your response? Your boss defines it?"

For participants this can be a mindset shift of an unaware thinking pattern that's difficult to grasp. I first came across it when reading Stephen Covey's The Seven Habits of Highly Effective People. With Habit 1, Be Proactive, he addresses the mindset of "someone or something is responsible for my situation, not me". It can be seen in people's language, for example when leaving a meeting early they might say, "I have to go now", but don't they mean they are choosing to go. Choosing one priority over another. Being responsible means being "Response Able", being able to choose your reaction.

In the language of Fred Kofmans "Conscious Business", conscious employees take ownership for their lives. We don't want to sleepwalk through what we are doing.

We may well have difficult or toxic bosses, toxic teams, or a toxic culture. With low psychological safety, it can also be that the safest behavior is to be an Oyster.

But reflect on your own mindset and sense of responsibility. We can take our own personal leadership.

We don't get to decide what happens or when; we do get to decide how we respond.

22 MY ROAD TO DAMASCUS

Diversity and Inclusion (D&I) is a clear change management topic, achieving a company-wide behavioral change is not easy and D&I especially can be a polarizing topic.

While the need to overcome resistance is obvious, resistance can be found in surprising places; it can be unintentionally built into those who might consider themselves supporters. Let me explain.

Some 10 years ago when we started building our D&I strategy, we conducted a series of focus groups on gender diversity to understand people's views and their experiences. The approach was to run 3-hour focus groups for men and women-only groups and then replicate these for mixed groups. The first group I ran was a mixed group comprised equally of men and women. They were primarily senior managers, and over the 3 hours, a rich and revealing discussion ensued with real openness and inquiry into understanding the different experiences, perspectives, and issues.

I considered myself a positive supporter for gender diversity and believed our company to be a place of equal opportunity. What I was unprepared for were the stories of how differently women experienced this "equal opportunity" company. Many stories were shared like being expected to be the note taker or coffee server in meetings or being more frequently interrupted. The session ended with a group of people truly more informed and resolved for the company to be more inclusive. Like the Bible story of Paul on the Road to Damascus, my beliefs were transformed.

The next day, I repeated the process with a men only group. We finished early with the group, concluding there was no issue as we were an equal opportunity employer after all. They simply had no awareness; as white European men, they assumed their experience was what others experienced. They were the "dominant" in company culture, and they had difficulty seeing and empathizing with the plight of the "other." I realized I was not the only one; they also needed a Road to Damascus experience; otherwise, progress toward inclusion would be slow.

This focus group left a lasting impression on me. If the problem cannot be seen, then the problem cannot be solved. I had had a blindspot to the experience of the "other", in this case women, that needed revealing for me to be a helpful ally. However, I realized awareness is not enough; it also needed anchoring in day-to-day behavior. Listening to Shelly McNamara, Chief Equality & Inclusion Officer at P&G, she highlighted the importance of building awareness and creating a language and framework that keeps bias as an ever-present concern. She described how, often in meetings, they use language like "I may be biased about this, but this is what I think," where the awareness of bias is part of how they work.

The Sky Media Group has focused on how to encourage inclusion through its "Conscious Inclusion everyday" questions.

1. Ensure there is a mix - invite different people to be part of your project or meeting.
2. Invite everyone to join in the conversation - watch out who speaks
3. Deliberately seek out alternative perspectives - not just your go-to people
4. Ask people what would make them feel included – what helps them speak up
5. Get to know people who are not like you – find employees and groups different from you

While the climate towards D&I is much improved, it remains a solid change management topic that starts with building awareness and desire.

- How to create a "Road to Damascus" experience for those who need it?
- How to anchor this with language and tools that maintain awareness and curiosity that can fuel an inclusive culture?

23 GETTING CUSTOMER FOCUSED

When Jeff joined as CEO, his first priority was learning the business.

One Sunday afternoon, while sitting on his moored boat, he got chatting to the boat owner beside him and discovered he was a customer. Without disclosing his role, he quietly listened as the customer told horror stories about how he was treated, the poor quality of the product, the arrogance, and the lack of interest and respect. While it would be difficult for him to switch suppliers, he was seriously considering it.

Jeff was horrified and committed to taking this to the management team meeting the next Monday.

But rather than grabbing the need to act, the management team pushed back and blamed the customer for the problems. Jeff realized the challenge was much deeper and would not be solved overnight.

The normal place to start would be communicating a new customer focus vision, quoting stats on the difficulty of getting new customers vs keeping existing ones and establishing some new metrics and incentives. However, Jeff started in a very different place, with himself.

Sitting with his assistant he set her the goal of making sure 60% of his time each week would be with customers or on customer topics. She needed to ensure he dramatically reduced his time on internal discussions.

His next action was to ask some customers if he could borrow a desk and sit in their offices to become more familiar with their company. This raised eyebrows but the customers were happy to loan Jeff a desk. Each time he visited, the curiosity of the customer's employees drew Jeff into many discussions about the customer's applications, the problems they were solving, and where the product was falling short.

Jeff's immediate reduction in internal availability and increased visibility at customers disrupted the management team. In team discussions, Jeff's knowledge of how the customer saw things and what opportunities there were, exposed how isolated the leadership team had become.

One by one, the other management team members also started to make similar changes.

Jeff could see the first step in his plan in becoming customer focused was working.

As change leaders, we can consider different ways to lead change rather than the well-worn path of the PowerPoint slide deck.

24 NOTHING IS THAT IMPORTANT

Nothing is that important that it is worth getting hurt over.

This was our Head of Health & Safety's screen saver.

It's sad to say but too many workplace accidents are because employees feel a commitment to their job or have a desire to be helpful. I remember the maintenance manager at the factory where I worked fell through the roof; he didn't wait for the safety harness because he felt he was holding up the next production shift. The factory was shut down for several days while the investigation was concluded.

To quote the sign a construction company uses at all their sites, "Nothing you do today on this site will be as important as going home to your family and loved ones." BP was trying to find a way for their safety training to stick; they decided at the end of every course, they would ask the participants to sign a photo of their family to remind them, "This is why I stay safe at work."

"Nothing is that important that it is worth getting hurt over."

However, whenever I read the screen saver, I always misread it. I thought of it in terms of the personal impact work can have on you from bullying, burnout and toxic workplaces. The statement is true for mental health & safety as much as physical health and safety.

In the Forbes article "Why Managers May Have a Bigger Mental-Health Impact Than Your Therapist". It references a report from The Workforce Institute, based on a survey of 3,400 employees and managers in 10 countries. It concluded that 60% of employees worldwide said their job is the biggest factor influencing their mental health. The conclusion was managers have just as much of an impact on people's mental health as their spouse (both 60%) and even more of an impact than their doctor (51%) or therapist (41%).

How long does it take to recover if someone is affected by burnout? It depends on which stage of burnout you're at and how long it takes for you to admit that there's a problem. On average, you'll usually start to see the first signs of recovery after a few months of treatment. Full recovery can take over a year. How long does it take to recover from bullying? How people respond to bullying can be as varied and complex as the bullying itself, but it can take years or even a lifetime. Seems to me prevention is far better than a cure.

This all begs the question, "What can managers do to use their power to benefit themselves and their employees?" As an arctic explorer will tell you, "Look after your huskies, and they'll look after you". Your very survival is dependent on your sled dogs pulling you to civilization.

I cannot imagine a time when hard work is not a key ingredient to success, but if you want to give your life, then join the army. In business…

"Nothing is that important that it is worth getting hurt over"

Talent

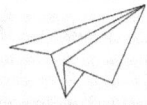

"Here's the thing. The challenge with talent management isn't to plot people onto a grid, it's to create movement in organizations and ensure we're enabling our employees to do the best work of their lives"

25 BUILDING A TALENT MINDSET

> *"We our separated from the secrets of success by an invisible barrier, our old mindset."*

In a dynamic and growing company, it was clear talent was important, but despite many innovative HR programs, something was holding them back. My task was to review the talent practices and make recommendations about how to bring them to the next level. During one of the senior leader interviews, I received the following warning. "Andy, be careful; if you make talent visible, everyone will try and grab them, and then how will you manage". My smile faded as I realized this was not a joke but a sincere comment born from hard-bitten experience. The issue was their talent mindset.

Like many of us, much of my talent management work has been implementing processes and structures that drive the behaviors to be lived in the organization, leading to the desired results. However, new processes without new mindsets are like old wine in new wineskins. While the right processes are important, they don't come alive until the right mindset is present. Mindsets are rarely explicit; they are filters through which we see the world. The term mindset was coined in the 1900s by psychology professor Peter Gollwitzer and brought to wider awareness in the nineties through Peter Senge's Fifth Discipline. Recently resurfacing through the work of Carol Dweck.

High-performing companies have leaders who possess a talent mindset. A positive talent mindset consists of several key characteristics, for example...

- A deep conviction that better talent equals better performance
- Without talent, strategy cannot be realized
- The ability to articulate the evolving future talent needs for each part of the organization

- A sense of the gold standard, what good looks like
- A recognition that talent belongs to the organization, to be encouraged and shared
- Not settling for "who fits the requirements and how fast can they start" but building bench strength by hiring for headroom

We have seen in recent years a reappraising of what a constructive talent mindset includes, with a stronger emphasis on diversity and employee-led career movement and away from manager-led talent management.

If a talent mindset is important then how to build it? We are dealing with our beliefs, like a table with legs, the legs of experience hold the belief up. We cannot change something that is in our blind spot; to change our talent beliefs, we first need to surface our current talent mindset and the experiences that have built this. With the willingness to examine them, you can reappraise your experiences and build a new set of beliefs. Not everyone will be willing, but enough needs to be willing to build a consensus and a set of new norms that will permeate the fabric of the organization. As a good housekeeper will tell you, "You cannot clean the stairs from the bottom". It is a worthy ambition to create a groundswell or movement within an organization, but you will also need to work with the senior leaders as they will set the boundary of how far you can go.

There is no more powerful leverage point to transform a system than to change the mindset. Any company seeking to gain a competitive advantage through superior talent must install a talent mindset.

What is your talent mindset, and is it holding you back?

26 THE POLARITIES OF TALENT MANAGEMENT

My nephew came to me one Sunday afternoon.

"Uncle, you are a very wise and clever person."

That's true, I thought.

"I have a difficult problem for you," he continued, "if you cannot solve it, can I have an ice cream?"

"Yes, of course; what is it?" I asked, feeling confident.

Of course, the answer is obvious: but my nephew got his ice cream.

"I was thinking, is it more important to breath in or breath out, you can only choose one?"

In business, we are often confronted with questions or problems but overlook the possibility that it is not an either/or but could be a both/and, a polarity.

I first came across the idea of polarities when I met Barry Johnson some years ago. I learned about the polarities we see in business, like centralization and decentralization, change and stability, and how to respond to them.

In Talent Management, we are no less susceptible to polarities.

1. Focus on internal talent vs external talent
2. Manager led vs employee-led
3. Planned careers vs emergent careers
4. The chosen few vs the important many

5. Leader vs manager
6. Standardized processes vs differentiated processes
7. Focus on the individual vs focus on the team
8. Disclose succession plans or keep them secret

We might find thought leaders advocating the "right answer" or creating charts of the "old way" vs "new way". Are these problems solved or polarities that need managing? The either/or mindset can be somewhat reductive, as if things are very simple and certain.

Barry teaches that each pole of polarity has its upsides AND downsides; it helps if we map out the full picture of both poles, create a shared understanding, and then seek to gain the upsides of both.

Look back through the list above and ask yourself …

1. Which polarities are you managing right now?
2. Where do you stand on each?
3. Are you getting the upside of both poles while minimizing the downsides?

27 THE POWER OF TALENT FACTORIES

A study published in 2015 by Santa Clara University revealed of the 1500 largest US companies, a disproportionately large number of CEOs originated from a small number of high-profile firms, which they labeled CEO factories. These included companies like IBM, GE, and Johnson & Johnson, recognized for their ability to consistently identify, develop, and deploy talent. Talent that also overflows into the market.

High-performing companies can build their talent factory to enable sustainable performance and growth. But to build a capability, you need to understand it; you need effective and robust maps, models, and frameworks: a talent management process. It can help us describe what otherwise happens intuitively and do it more consciously or provide structure to what currently happens chaotically.

In ABB we developed and refined our own talent management process. It became the spine through which all our initiatives, tools and programs were anchored. It enabled us to build the shared talent mindset across the business. It falls into five phases.

1. Identify: Differentiating employees so decisions can be made on where to invest and take appropriate actions.
2. Commit: Aligning the company's and employees' expectations before investing significant resources.
3. Assess: Insight into individual needs rather than adopting a one-size-fits-all approach.
4. Develop: Investing in employee development, leader and functional.
5. Advance: Moving people to their next career step

Like many good things we do in HR, in the business of doing them, we can lose sight of the problem we are solving. Before embarking on talent management, it is essential to understand the specific problems and trends the organization is trying to address. This may include the need for new capabilities, identifying and retaining top talent, filling key positions, and developing talents faster. Talent management starts with a talent strategy, which comes from the overall business plan, a clear understanding of the current situation, and a focus on attracting, retaining, and developing the right people. Connecting the demand side and supply side of the talent equation. Be purposeful.

Finally, Talent Management is a collective effort, a team sport involving line managers, employees, and HR. It is essential to foster a strong partnership; it is not a process that can be delegated to any one group. A talent management process provides a common language and framework to address the needs underpinned by a shared talent mindset.

Time to build our Talent Factories.

28 LAUNCHING TALENT PROCESSES

Human Resources is a change management function. Every year, we run many programs and new processes that must be adopted to deliver impact. Interestingly, there does not seem to be well-established and clear best practices for how to set up and launch new processes and programs. After implementing many global HR projects, what would be my ten lessons?

1. Underestimating the change management - Comments like "let's not make a fuss", or "we'll let the HRBP's lead it", or "let's not overcomplicate it". These all end up being excuses for not taking the change management seriously and just throwing it over the wall.

2. Overlooking the stakeholder management - "This is our job, so no need to trouble them". The sponsors need to sponsor, it doesn't help keeping them out of the loop.

3. Thinking we know what's best - Not talking to the user or customer. Too much inside out and not enough outside in.

4. Lacking the science - Not going back to the research to understand what's behind it. Look towards evidence-based HR to avoid falling for fashions or the next cool thing. We might find some practices are based on questionable "science".

5. Not seeing the solution also has downsides - no solution is perfect; they don't just solve a problem, they also create new ones. The person who invented the car also invented the car crash (Paul Virilio). It's important to anticipate the challenges it will introduce and not be surprised.

6. Providing too little support material - I have often been told not to produce materials because "nobody will read it". It might seem wise to keep material simple on launch. Still, down the line, if you have too little documentation, it's hard for new managers,

employees, and future process owners to pick up and understand policies and processes.

7. Poor project management - Not putting in place a project manager and then managing it like a project. Casually changing scope and requirements without consideration for impact.
8. Lacking clear measures of success - How will we know we made things better? Thinking the talent process is the solution and forgetting it's what people do that's the solution. We should not lose sight of the purpose.
9. Being dishonest about reasons for change - Why are we really changing? To solve a business need or for new HR leaders to put their stamp on things. If we become bored with the old process, we should resist the need for change for our own ego.
10. Not spending as much time embedding as launching - Lots of effort put into the launch needs to be balanced with the follow-through and embedding.

Designing elegant tools and processes may be satisfying, but the final measures are adoption and impact. I have spent over 30 years launching projects and built a launch pad to set projects up for success.

Be a good sponsor, invest time into planning, you won't regret it.

29 MANAGING THE RECRUITMENT FACTORY

"Nothing is more important than hiring and developing people. At the end of the day, you bet on people, not on strategies."

We sat in Gabriel's office; it was a summer day, and the office window was open; we could hear the howl of a Ferrari F1 car on the Ferrano test circuit. I was lost for a moment in a reverie, like a childhood dream. My focus returned to the topic at hand: talent.

"So, what is your biggest challenge regarding talent?" I asked.

Gabriel was the Head of Talent Management for Ferrari; without a word, he reached onto the floor and slammed a huge pile of CVs onto his desk.

"Attracting talent," he said, "is not our problem; getting the right talent is."

"Everybody wants to work for a cool company like Ferrari, but finding the right talent is difficult."

Talent acquisition can be split into two main aspects: attraction and selection. Attraction is about generating a bench of potential candidates. Selection is the process of converting the potential candidates into the final hire. Using the analogy of business functions, it's a factory operation with a marketing front end. What links them together is meeting the needs of the business while creating a positive candidate experience.

Attraction as the marketing front end, is about reaching the right people, differentiating your message, and creating visibility. This also needs to be partnered with hunting, actively finding the right talent not just waiting for them to come. I believe great recruiters are closer in attitude to great salespeople than typical HR. They know the market and competitors, know the product they are selling (the role) and can sell to the customer (applicants). They don't waste time with those who will never buy, demonstrate persistence, and are great closers. But like in business, sales are not enough; a company also needs a clear position in the market and awareness with the people they try to reach. Productivity can be lost by sorting through large numbers of applicants who are not suitable; they don't fit the role or the culture of the company.

Selection as the factory produces hires and has a different set of challenges. It's about efficiency and maximizing capacity with the need for accuracy to reliably and consistently select the right people. How to organize recruitment for it to be most effective? Like any production line that handles variety, the loading needs analyzing an understanding of volumes and frequency. Should you organize around geography, business, or specialism? Like in factories there can be the temptation to solve the selection problem with technology without fundamentally solving the basics of the process. While technology can help, it can be an island of efficiency in a sea of chaos. Driven by unclear requirements, starting and stopping the hiring process or a drive to save cost but overspending on search firms.

With talent acquisition we are in a partnership, and the manager holds 51% of the responsibility. It doesn't matter what you do if managers trip up the process, so any solution needs to be jointly committed to.

What is your challenge, the factory or the marketing front end?

30 RECRUITMENT POSTMORTEM

"You look a bit low" Richard observed

"Yea despite the changes we have made to the HR operating model the Division President told us the last recruitment was a disaster" I replied.

Richard was my Lean Six Sigma coach, and we were working on embedding the HR transformation.

"There is always something to learn about how we turn frustration into a learning," he said, "let's speak with data and not jump to conclusions."

"What do you suggest?" I asked.

"We should do a postmortem on the recruitment. Fact-based, not opinion. Let's interview the key players, reconstruct the timeline, and see what conclusions and recommendations come out."

Six weeks later we reported back to the Division President and his team. We went over what we had found...

- Confusion over who was the right recruiter to contact
- Poor start to the process as the hiring manager was too busy for the kick-off meeting, causing rework
- The recruiter acquiesced to the manager's demand instead of following the process
- Internal candidate blocked, unwilling to release from current role
- Initial offer not competitive
- Lost two external candidates in succession after offer acceptance because the hiring manager did not keep in touch

TALENT

- Internal candidate eventually appointed
- Eight months' time to fill

The report back triggered a very productive conversation with the leadership team.

The Division President summarised the discussion.

"First, I appreciated this fact-based discussion rather than us flying off with all our opinions. Second, while HR still has some areas for improvement, the biggest task is on our side; if we don't play our role as managers, we cannot expect the process to work."

This was not the last time I applied this approach. When managers judge our HR delivery based purely on perceptions, often a bad experience, we don't like it. So, equally, we should not judge our delivery based on our own anecdotal evidence. We should use facts and objective data to put delivery performance into context. In HR we are often working in partnership with managers, it helps a lot if we speak with data and hold up the mirror.

What opportunities do you have for continuous improvement, turning frustration into learning?

31

THE BARBARA EXPERIENCE

I was glad to have Barbara on the team. We often chatted when I passed by her desk; she proudly showed me her work on our learning management system. Something well appreciated by the leadership and employees alike.

When our Head of Talent left, Barbara applied for the position. It's great to see the enthusiasm and ambition in employees, even if they stand no chance of getting the job. We were looking for someone with competence to lead the function forward.

When it came to the interviews Barbara was on the list, I felt a duty to include her. Walking into the interview, I didn't think we would need the whole hour; I was probably going through the motions.

As usual, we started by walking through her CV, and I was surprised to see she had been the Head of Talent and Development for a large call center.

"I was there three years," she told me, "Until they outsourced it to a low-cost country, and I was laid off. That's how I ended up here".

My interest was piqued and I became curious to know what kind of talent work she had done. Over the next 40 minutes Barbara talked about the challenges of turnover, productivity, team leader quality, talent identification. She explained how the issues had been tackled. The results were impressive, so I probed further into what HER contribution had been. Her personal impact came screaming back.

I am embarrassed to say I thought I knew her, but my perception of the person in front of me was transformed. I had massively underestimated her capabilities.

She became my lead candidate and then finally the successful applicant.

As a Talent Manager too often we observe managers who have made their mind up about people despite the absence or presence of data.

In our busy days, we may not have time to get to know everyone, but at least during the interview, we should give them our full attention with a truly open mind. We want to ensure we make high quality people decisions.

In retrospect, I can confirm Barbara delivered. She moved on some years later, and I observed with some delight to see her progression.

Can you remember a time when you changed your mind about someone?

32   THE 8TH WASTE

> *"Brain the size of a planet, and they've got me opening doors"*
> **Marvin, The Paranoid Android**
> **The Hitchhikers Guide to The Galaxy**

The horror of Marvin's existence is that no task he is given occupies even the tiniest fraction of his vast intellect. As funny as the character is, it expresses something about the sad state of wasted potential.

The Toyota Production System (TPS) introduced the concept of waste. They defined the 7 wastes (defects, motion, waiting, inventory, transportation, over-processing, over-production). But there is an 8th waste - the waste of human potential; it is the waste of unused talent and ingenuity.

Japanese industry innovated the idea of employee involvement. Those doing the work are best placed to identify and develop solutions to eliminate waste. As noted by Amy Edmondson, Professor of Leadership at Harvard Business School, they were early advocates for psychological safety to enable employees to speak up about problems and ideas for improvement. The most extreme was the Andon cord at Toyota, authorizing every employee on the assembly line to immediately halt production when they notice a problem or defect.

The 8th waste is personal. The frustration of wanting to contribute but not given the chance. Having your ideas ignored or being passed over for a bigger challenge. We want to give our best, contribute, make a difference, and grow.

The 8th waste is also a talent manager's concern. As Talent Managers, we exist to unlock the potential of people's lives and create an environment where people can give their best so the company can achieve its goals.

There are many solutions available to realize this. We have skills management, talent marketplaces, and learning platforms, but like Lean Manufacturing, to make it work requires a different way of thinking. A Talent Mindset. It needs managers, employees, and HR to work in partnership.

With all the effort this requires, does it even matter?

We are leaving something on the table which we cannot afford to do. Konosuke Matsushita, Founder of Panasonic & Technics, put it best…

> *"Business, we know, is now so complex and difficult, the survival of firms so hazardous in an environment increasingly unpredictable, competitive and fraught with danger, that their continued existence depends on the day-to-day mobilization of every ounce of intelligence."*

Let's hope our people are not Marvin's, left to just "opening doors".

33 THE PROBLEM WITH 360 FEEDBACK

"We judge ourselves by our intentions;
others judge us by our actions."

It was late at night, and I was still pouring over my 360° leadership report: all twenty-five pages of it. As Head of Talent Management, I both wanted and needed to take this seriously, but I was struggling. I simply couldn't get any value from all the charts showing the distribution of ratings from colleagues and team members and comparisons to my own ratings. Frustrated and desperate, I finally tore out just three pages, my ratings compared to my boss, my top and bottom five displayed behaviors, and the free text comments about strengths and weaknesses. Armed with these pages, I could create my action plan.

360° feedback, also known as multi-rater feedback, is a process of combining self-assessment with the feedback of others, typically based on a set of defined behaviors. First used in the military to assess suitability for officer roles, it has become prevalent in business. It is currently going through a renewal with the advent of AI augmenting the approach. Life without feedback is lonely, and the challenge gets bigger as we become more senior. Without feedback, self-perception or "self-deception" is all we have. A 360 provides a structured way to gather feedback from the very people we work with, the ones who know us best. Different contributors have different abilities to provide reliable feedback. The leader's manager probably has the best view of driving results or strategic orientation behaviors. Peers are well placed to judge behaviors around collaboration and teamwork. Direct reports are best placed to judge team leadership or people development behaviors.

While a 360 tool is simple to deploy it should not be forgotten its purpose is for development and behavior change. It is a misconception to believe that individuals will automatically change once they receive "open and honest" feedback. From my experience, without a well-thought-through feedback process, all too often, you find leaders explaining away the improvement areas. Feedback is the death of self-image; it often speaks to the blind spot of our Johari window. We are all human, and the death of self-image can threaten our self-esteem and create resistance to change. Therefore, even with willing leaders, we must consider the feedback process carefully.

It starts with providing insight so the leader can say, "I get it." This is not achieved by simply handing out the report or reading it out loud. It is more than information-giving; it is about awareness and understanding of their impact and how others perceive them. But this is only the beginning. The real value comes from the desire to take action: "I will do something about it". How to connect to what motivates them, what are their goals and how the feedback can support them. If their ambition is to be more strategic, but the assessment indicates they are acting tactically, we can agree on something to improve that is important to them.

With the insight and commitment to act, leaders should not be left scrambling for resources. Come armed with your own ideas for development actions, so they can leave the feedback session telling us "I have the resources I need" and "I have the opportunity to practice". Lastly, ensure each leader has an accountability partner. "I have someone who is my conscience" who will provide reinforcement and hold them accountable. This is where the leader's manager can play a powerful role in coaching for development.

Let's not underestimate the challenge of effective 360° feedback. I hope your leaders won't find themselves struggling late at night trying to figure out what to do with their next 360 report, as I once did.

34

WHAT ABOUT 70:20:10?

"We don't learn from experience. We learn from reflecting on the experience."
John Dewey

I have been mulling over the 70:20:10 concept. It's easy to push the responsibility for the 70% on-the-job learning to managers and employees with an expectation that the 70% is the most effective way for people to learn.

However, we might be doing ourselves and our people a disservice by de-emphasizing off-the-job training in favor of on-the-job. We might be sending the message that we think they get 70% of their learning just by doing their job? Of course, we don't leave them totally on their own, so we give managers lists of activities that they need to turn into something for on-the-job learning. Unsurprisingly few do anything with it because it is not so easy.

The 70:20:10 concept emerged from a 1987 study by the Center for Creative Leadership (CCL). They surveyed 191 successful North American executives (including 2 women), identifying 616 key learning events, which were categorized as Challenging Assignments: Other People; Course Work; and Personal Hardships. The Personal Hardships were removed (17.5%) even though they were a powerful way to learn it's not something you can engineer. This left the split of 70, 20, and 10, which has become the point of reference for learning strategies.

It's a surprisingly small sample that has set fire to widespread adoption. It should be noted that the 70% was challenging assignments not just any work experience. The research doesn't address what is challenging, nor the duration and intensity. Was it sufficient, or did it draw from theories and models learned from training courses?

Experience is powerful; it is personal and engaging but not sufficient; we also need to extract the value from those experiences, build new mental models and behaviors, and enable the application of that learning, as Kolb showed us through his learning cycle. In simple terms…

- Expose
- Extract
- Apply

So, if we leave the 70% to managers or employees, how easy is it to design the on-the-job learning? Does it require any expertise? Can anyone do it? Is there is nothing to it? Is it just common sense?

If 70% of learning really is on the job, how come our learning budgets and teams spend 100% of their time on the 10% off the job?

- What are your assumptions about 70:20:10?
- What are you communicating to the managers and employees?
- What changes should you make?

35 THE PASSION CONCEPT

"Andy, that was very inspiring and a breath of fresh air." I had just finished a session for the global HR community on handling change. We were in the middle of a dramatic transformation, restructuring the organization, and many employees felt uncertain about their jobs. The compulsion was to grab at any opportunity. Understandable in the short-term but maybe not so good for the longer-term career. We wanted to bring a more constructive and empowering perspective, and this came through the idea of the "sweet spot".

The sweet spot is achieved when you can align your passion, your competence, and the organization's needs. It's in the sweet spot where you feel the motivation, engagement, and ability to fully perform and keep performing. Adapted from the Japanese concept of Ikigai, discovering your purpose through exploring the intersection of what you love, what you're good at, what the world needs, and what you can be paid for.

But like ikigai the passion concept also can evolve. It changes over time, and that is okay. As we change, our sweet spot changes as well. What once felt right might not feel right two years down the road. In Spencer Johnson's 1998 book "Who Moved My Cheese?", he articulated the importance of going where the "cheese" is. When it's gone, the role becomes a chore; you are unlikely to give your best or feel engaged. In fact, every day can be energy-draining.

Leaders carry an extra responsibility during times of change to bring their teams through the change process without diluting the employee's self-responsibility and ownership. How can they help them find the right place or discover a passion in the changed role?

For the 1:1 conversations between leader and team member here is a list of questions to encourage each person to reflect as part of their journey.

- How do you see your role changing?
- What are your strengths and key competencies?
- What are you passionate about in your work?
- Where does your future career passion lie?
- What opportunities does the change in role provide?
- What career options are available?
- What opportunities are there by being involved in the transformation?

36 HOW IS YOUR SHARE PRICE?

My friend was very frustrated with his career.

After investing in his development, taking an international assignment, and participating in a series of special projects, he could not find his next career step in the organization. He was perpetually overlooked for other candidates.

"But Andy, I don't get it," he said, "my performance ratings have been high, my leadership assessment shows strong competencies, and yet I don't progress."

"John" I said, "you miss the third the factor"

"What's that?" he asked.

"Your Share Price"

"What on earth do you mean?".

Like a company share price, I see people's careers seem to rise based on positive perceptions or equally falter based on skewed perceptions. I have seen leadership teams fall in love with talent (like a shiny new toy). The new, fresh talent emerges, and they become someone well perceived and talent to promote, which everyone feels good about doing.

The art and science of good talent management comes down to making high-quality people decisions. Matching analysis with judgment. While "the cream will rise to the top" it sometimes needs a little help to rise. This is especially true for advancing diversity.

As hiring managers be self-aware of your biases and balance head and heart decision making. Are you being seduced by talents who like to be visible in meetings but overlook those who expect their results to speak for them? The best managers of talent stay committed to their talent as they develop, whether their share price goes up or down.

As individuals, be aware, perceptions matter. In the HBR article "Savvy Self-Promotion," they address the topic that success at work depends on not just being competent and likable but also being seen as such. For some of us we need to become comfortable with managing our visibility. The article has valuable tips with the caution to not replace performance with self-promotion.

Postscript

What was the solution for my colleague? In my view, his aspirations were realistic, and he would have performed well in the roles he was targeting; however, in the end, leaving the organization was his way forward. He joined another global company and thrived, earning greater responsibility and increasingly senior roles. Not everyone stays forever, but let's ensure we use good talent management so that the right people advance and we don't lose talent unnecessarily.

How is your share price?

37 EVERYBODY'S FREE TO WEAR SUNSCREEN

As I get later in my career, I am frequently asked for my career advice. In these moments, I am reminded of the essay "Everybody's Free (To Wear Sunscreen)." It always connects me back to maintaining a sense of perspective that comes from a lived life.

As in the essay, this is what I learned about making those difficult career decisions, my advice has no basis more reliable than my own meandering experience...

I will dispense this advice now...

- Do it for yourself - is the opportunity what you want to do, or what others want you to do? You can be pushed towards opportunities; at that moment, it can be quite a compliment, but beware, are you taking it for the good of others and not necessary for you? In the end, everyone else will move on; you need to be sure it is best for you.
- Do your due diligence - not all good opportunities are good. Some can be a "poisoned chalice"; it may not be a role where you can succeed and won't lead you to the future you desire.
- Not all moves are up - those who have advanced far in their career have often taken sideways career steps in order to get to their desired destination. Career paths are rarely straight and linear, they are rather more a winding road. I have often been asked for structured career maps and plans, but in practice, very few people's careers follow this kind of linear and logical route.
- Collect experiences - Taking your time in your career can be good. Don't get there too early and not be ready. Looking back, I can now say that jumping career steps left gaps in my experience that I missed later on. Learning, building your experiences, plugging the gaps, and seeing business differently are good.

- The timing isn't always your choosing - I was offered a global role at exactly the time I was really making progress in my current role; it felt like the offer came a year early. In the end, I did not regret the timing; however, I realized roles follow a predictable pattern - Year 1, get started; Year 2, get going; Year 3, really make the impact.
- More opportunities will come - if you are good then it is very likely that another opportunity will come in the future. This won't be the last one you are offered.
- It's 50/50 - your choices are half chance; when you can't decide between two options if you are really struggling with which one to choose and you have discussed and analyzed the options and still cannot decide, then both are good, and there is no wrong choice. Decisions sometimes are 50/50, not right and wrong.
- Tightrope or field - how do you see the journey of life? Is it a tightrope where each decision is critical? Make the wrong one, and you fall off the tightrope to your death, never to return? I think life is more like a field; there is much room for options and different paths, and getting off track is much harder than you think.
- Choose your boss as well as your job - When you take a new role, see whom you are going to work for. The boss makes all the difference to your work life – one who steers you on the correct path or limits your performance.
- Don't chase the money - jumping roles for more money is dangerous. The money rarely mitigates an unfulfilling role.

Be careful whose advice you buy but be patient with those who supply it.

But trust me on the sunscreen.

Change

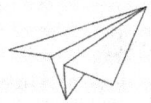

"Progress is impossible without change. And those who cannot change their minds cannot change anything."
George Bernard Shaw

38 CAN WE CHANGE?

In Oxford in 1954, Roger Bannister broke the 4-minute time barrier for running the mile.

Nobody had run a sub-4-minute mile before, and in fact, many attempts had been made in the previous 12 months. The Australian John Landy had come close many times and started to believe it was impossible. In fact, many had said a sub-4-minute mile was beyond the capability of the human frame, and to attempt it runs the risk of heart failure or asphyxiation.

Within a month, Bannister's record had been broken by Landy, and in the subsequent months, a flood of other runners achieved the goal. Why was the record suddenly possible to break? In my view the barrier had proven to be a mental barrier as much as a physical barrier.

Businesses can be conservative and risk-averse. We have probably all experienced being told something is not possible.

We discovered during the pandemic how swift and dramatic change was possible. Why? I believe there were some great ingredients of change gifted to us that we now need to take care we learn from…

- The need for change was compelling - The nature of the pandemic and its consequences were severe. In many countries, when they did act, they did it quickly. How can we articulate a similar compelling need for the changes we want to make now?
- The alignment between leaders and employees was high - Everyone saw the same problem and was affected in the same way. It was a very levelling situation. As companies continue to evolve, how to create the same alignment in the future with the same stake in the change?

- There was deliberate and frequent communication - Employees felt well informed by the CEO and their direct line managers - employees preferred communication channels. Are we prepared for this same level of communication effort?
- There was a commitment and effort to make it work for our jobs and the survival of the business - Fuelled in part by the excitement and adrenaline of something new and novel. Like the day school is unexpectedly cancelled due to snow. Everyone moved along the adoption curve together. How can this be replicated?
- There was collaboration across boundaries - It created patterns of collaboration that had not previously existed to solve problems, there is nothing like an external threat to bring people together. Can we maintain this internal collaboration?
- Flexibility remained, based on the emerging situation - Decisions were made quickly but always in the knowledge this decision might need to be revisited. In business, we treat change as somehow a once and for all decision. How can we maintain a more experimental and agile approach to change?

The 2020 pandemic may be a distant memory, but it is important not to throw away the learning so we can replicate those conditions, make successful changes, and run our "sub-4-minute mile".

39 ONE FIRM SPOT

> *"Give me a firm spot on which to stand and a lever long enough, and I will move the earth."*
> **Archimedes**

Moving the earth requires more than a lever but also a firm place to stand. During times of change, our challenge is finding our "firm spot to stand on".

In my career, I have been part of many kinds of businesses and many kinds of changes - I have been acquired, divested, merged, and restructured. Each time I never knew how it would affect me and those around me. During such times many of us face uncertainty. As a change manager and leader, what advice would I give to my colleagues (and myself) in handling organizational change?

- Be a student of strategy – Seek to understand what the change is about, why it is important, why we need to change now, how it will help the business and what would happen if we didn't change? Some strategies we like, others we like less. Every strategy has upsides and downsides; try to see the full picture. I call this process making peace with the change. Accepting it is part of the well-known Moss-Kanter change curve.

- Focus on what you can influence – Some change is welcomed; we initiate change in our own professional and personal lives. The real problem with change is control, i.e., the difference between what concerns us and what we can influence and what concerns us and what we cannot influence. Don't complain and sit around endlessly discussing; focus on what you can influence, not what you cannot. When focusing on what you cannot influence often means neglecting what you can. Hence, your influence will shrink. Focus on the things you can do something about. With this, you stay positive and increase your circle of influence.

- Be clear on what is not changing – Avoid being overwhelmed; not everything changes, and you are not losing everything familiar. Identify what will remain and is staying intact so you can focus on adapting to the changes without fear of losing everything you know.
- Stay flexible – "Unless you are prepared to give up something valuable, you will never be able to truly change at all because you'll be forever in the control of things you can't give up." Don't try and hold back the tide; maintain a constant interest in learning and what can be learned from the changes. A change often brings something new, something to learn and grow from. Being inflexible in a world that is VUCA (Volatile, Uncertain, Complex, Ambiguous) will only make us stressed and miserable.
- Passion concept – Spencer Johnson wrote in 1998 a very helpful short book called "Who Moved My Cheese?" I like to think of work as an intersection between what we do well, what we love to do, and what the organization needs. The "sweet spot" is achieved when you can align your passion and competence with the job requirements. You feel the motivation, engagement, and ability to fully perform. My personal experience has led me to believe opportunities will come, but we should seek roles in the "sweet spot," not just any available role.
- Take ownership – Leaders carry an extra responsibility during times of change to communicate and bring their teams through the change process. However, it is still important to take ownership of your own change journey and avoid a victim mindset.

Changes will surely come, and my commitment is to find my "firm spot to stand on." what about you?

40 CHANGE RESISTANCE IS IMPORTANT

"Resistance is the first step to change"
Louise Hay

It was Friday afternoon, and I had just finished a half-day Just-In-Time (JIT) Awareness session. It was part of a transformation of the manufacturing operations and was what we called a sheep dip session; everyone got to go regardless of role or need. Of course, this meant there were plenty of prisoners and passengers. Each session often became a battle, with participants arguing against what we were presenting.

After running two sessions a day for a week, I was really exhausted. My boss came swanning in at the end of the Friday session and casually commented with a smile, "That was a lively session". OK, so he got both barrels, I was tired and I unloaded my frustrations. My boss was a little taken aback but stayed quiet. After a pause, he asked me one question.

"What if they stayed silent and then walked out at the end? Do you think that would be better?"

I was stopped in my tracks.

I could immediately see the problem with a silent (and passive) group. You see, their questions and comments reflected something that I was overlooking. This kind of energy showed they were engaged and that they cared. What we were trying to do mattered.

We can call it resistance, but that's part of the change; we need to wrestle with what's new, with the emotions, the ideas, and implications; we might be giving something up that's important to us or at least think we are. We may not have seen the opportunity to learn or do something new, something more interesting and fulfilling.

Productive skepticism drives successful change more than compliance. Employees who are willing to question or be skeptical of a change can improve it with constructive criticism; sadly, they are more likely to be labeled as resistors. Compliant employees, who largely take directions, are not as effective at driving change success.

Not all resistance is good, some resistance is self-inflicted and unnecessary because we have not anticipated the poor positioning, creating misunderstanding. With some pre-thought and planning, it can be avoided.

Over time, I became more skillful in handling the group's questions and objections. I started to appreciate the engagement and its importance. I realized as a leader, we need to create an environment where team members can speak up, give voice to objections, and have the time to deal with them.

Change is emotional, not just logical. Resistance is inevitable, a natural reaction. We all deal with change differently, some passively and some actively.

It might not be easy, but be thankful for the engagement.

41 POLARITIES OF CHANGE COMMUNICATION

"For every action, there is an equal and opposite reaction."
Newton's Third Law.

Daryl Conner was the first to use the idea of the burning platform. It was based on the 1988 Piper Alpha disaster and the interview with a survivor, who, against all his training, jumped off the platform into the ice-cold sea and survived. When asked why, he said, "I chose possible death over certain death". He jumped because he felt he had no choice— the price of staying on the platform was too high.

Since then, the case for change has been based on articulating today's problems and how we must change and move towards a bright new future. The world is not that simple. The more pressure put into advocating the change, the more resistance can increase. In the end we might brutalize the organization into changing.

Barry Johnson introduced me to the idea of polarities. We treat many topics as problems to solve, either this or that. In business many topics are interdependent polarities, both/and. Like breathing in and out, there is no one right answer; it is about managing the dynamics between the two. Centralization - decentralization, focus on the individual - focus on the team, etc.

One of these polarities is change and stability. Smart change communication balances the drive towards change by providing the firm a place to stand from what is not changing.

For every upside of a change, there are also downsides. No solution is perfect. There are upsides for every downside of the current state; not everything about today is wrong.

Advocates of a vision can sound like crusaders; resisters of vision can sound like traditionalists. We all see the truth, but only partially. The crusaders and traditionalists might see the same picture, but each only sees one-half of it.

Effective change seeks to get the upside of the new without losing the upside of the present.

Early in my career, I learned to "Value the past while looking to the future."

So, here are four possible steps for how we communicate the change...

1. Acknowledge the positive things of today (stability +ve)
2. Point out some of the obvious risks of doing things the new way (change -ve)
3. Articulate the downsides if we don't change (stability -ve)
4. Benefits if we go ahead and make this change (change +ve)

42 CASCADE MEETINGS FOR SUCCESSFUL CHANGE

There is a temptation to communicate directly to all employees.

It has its place but it can also build resistance in some important groups rather than winning them over. At a time when you need your middle managers to be champions for change, bypassing them with direct communication disempowers and dilutes their role. Is there a better way that engages everyone?

Cascade team briefing is a disciplined way of transmitting information down through the organization's management chain. Starting with the most senior team, using a standard briefing pack, they hold a two-way discussion - it's a good way for teams to really digest the changes and it also enables feedback up through the organization. It is a truly participative approach as it provides each team (virtual, hybrid, face-to-face) the opportunity for discussion, questions, and feedback.

These are five reasons why I would consider it good change management and worth the effort.

1. Active and visible executive leadership and sponsorship – Research shows that one of the most critical success factors for successful change is the visible commitment and engagement of the senior leader. As the cascade process starts with the leadership team, they get to role model the approach.
2. Hear it from your manager - When it comes to change, studies show 67% of employees rate their direct manager as the preferred change communication channel. Managers are best placed to contextualize the message, build support, and mitigate resistance.

3. Employee involvement and participation - Involving and engaging all employees builds understanding and ownership, vital for successful implementation.
4. What it means for me – Some years ago, when the company I worked for launched its Integrity & Compliance initiative, it was rolled out through a team briefing cascade. In my team we thought it was not a topic relevant to us. However, we ran the session anyway, and as we worked through the material, there was a joint realization it was, in fact, relevant to us, and we had actions to take. This is a powerful aspect of these team sessions; discussion gives time to digest the topic and see what it means.
5. Signals something new by doing it in a new way - The team briefing in many organizations is also an excellent opportunity to start a new way of communicating and collaborating. Leaders steer the discussion but let their team members do most of the talking, reflecting the aspired culture and leadership style.

Our ambition is to make change successfully using methods that work, ensuring we engage everyone as change champions and avoid disempowering the managers we rely on to lead.

43 THEY LEFT ME OUT OF THE COFFEE CLUB

"My body travelled very fast, but my heart took a little longer"
Mr Gruber, Paddington Bear.

We were implementing a shared services organization. A lot of work had gone into the planning, and now, as part of the implementation, we were running a series of large-scale workshops. They brought together people from across many sites and offices who were now part of the larger shared services team.

I was the facilitator but also ran a session on handling change and the importance of finding your "firm spot to stand on" while things are changing around you.

A lady sought me out during the coffee break. She was excited and thanked me for the session.

"I am glad to be part of something bigger," she explained. "I can see it will provide me with professional opportunities and career growth."

Then, her face changed.

"It's not all been good," she told me, "When the announcement of the new shared services came and that I would be part of it, something strange happened. It was clear I was no longer going to belong to the local team, so they left me out of the coffee club."

"It was horrible. I felt isolated and abandoned."

"Today has been so important for me to be able to join my new team and feel at home here."

Business is a human enterprise and people are not just hands and brains but also feelings. When winning hearts and minds, it's not just acceptance. It's also about building identity and belonging. Social belonging is a fundamental human need, hardwired into our DNA. Exclusion is harmful because it actually hurts: the sensation is akin to physical pain; it's a sting we've probably all experienced at one time or another.

When we manage change, we manage many transitions, the journey from one place to another. In the rush to get there, let's not leave people behind.

44 HRBP INFLUENCING WITH IMPACT

It was the final day of the Influencing with Impact program.

Jennifer, my client on the course and an Human Resources Business Partner (HRBP), had a challenge with one of the managers she supported. She wasn't getting through; he was ignoring her, and the programs she implemented were not getting traction. How could she change this? How could she influence her client?

We had learned the skills of influencing, "You can't influence that which you don't understand." I had spent time understanding the situation but also the person, what was important to Jennifer and her client? What levers were there for me to influence a course of action?

We sat down together in the breakout room. I think we were both a little anxious, me because I wanted to be successful; for her, she hoped I had something worthwhile to offer. This problem was important.

I had understood something about her Hilltop, her view on the world. While she was relationship-orientated, her logical side was much stronger, making her quite structured and detail-orientated. Her client (the manager), however, was a classic tough battler, status-driven, results-focused, and impatient. It had become evident she needed to adjust her approach.

Using a logical approach, I reasoned out a way for her to solve the problem…

It was clear meeting in his office created an unequal power distance; she was on his turf, and he controlled it. My first advice was to instead hold the meetings on neutral ground. She didn't have her own office, but she could engineer to meet in a conference room when he visited her site.

Second, prepare and run the meetings as short, sharp, and business-like as possible. Being methodical was not working; she needed to avoid unnecessary explanations and get down to business.

Third, use peer pressure and data, create a league table of initiatives, and motivate him by showing which manager was being most successful or quickest. This will appeal to his competitive side.

Fourth, her arguments were too much about doing the right thing for his people; this was not high on his priorities, and instead, she needed to show how it benefited him and his goals.

Jennifer got very excited; she realized she had been approaching him how she liked to be convinced, not what mattered to him. She could see the logic of a different approach and how this was the right thing to do to reach her goal.

We caught up a few weeks later.

"How have you got on?" I inquired

"Andy, it's not been easy," she replied, "but it has been a big step forward. We have had a breakthrough and started to find mutual respect. Now that credibility is established, we see the benefit of our different styles complementing our strengths. I now have a platform to work much more successfully"

How are you getting on influencing your clients?

45

HE BOUGHT A CARVING KNIFE

"You can't influence that which you don't understand"
Kevin Martin

Understanding people is at the core of influencing people to change. Our life experience builds us up layer by layer, creating our own unique Hilltop on the world. How do you understand people's Hilltops? Well, we are constantly broadcasting our Hilltops; we just need to listen. I was attending a change management training. We sat in a trio; John was the client; he would tell me what he bought, and I needed to understand his Hilltop. My role was as the consultant, asking the questions, and Janet's job was to observe and provide us with feedback. I had done my preparation; I had my questions, and I was ready to practice.

"So, what did you buy?" I asked. "A carving knife." replied John. My face was a picture; I was stumped. How can something so simple, maybe even trivial, be the subject of a fifteen-minute diagnosis practice that would reveal the person's Hilltop? I felt frustrated, even a bit angry, because this was probably a waste of time, and I was to be robbed of the learning I was expecting. OK, I thought, go for it and trust the process. If I finish in 2 minutes, then so be it. Start with the facts,

"Where did you buy it…. how long have you been looking for a knife…. how much did it cost? "£200" replied John

What…wait…. just a minute…."£200" I repeated back.

I started to get curious. Who spends that much money on a kitchen knife? "What do you like about it?" I asked.

"Oh well, the blade has a beautiful pattern on it from the steel manufacturing process; I love how balanced it is when you hold it in your hand, and I love the feel of the handle; it has been carefully profiled."

I noted each point down.

"Which is your favorite?" I asked. "Mmmm"… he thought for a minute…..another minute passed…he was deep in thought. "The balance of the knife." He replied

"Why is that important to you?" "Well, if you are going to do something, you need to do it properly."

Bingo. Looking back to that moment, I was glad for the simplicity of the purchase because it taught me an important lesson. I uncovered an important drive and value to which I needed to connect to influence change. At the end, the observer Janet said, "I could have saved you a lot of money; the knives in the supermarket are just as good and a tenth of the price. John went quiet, then slowly turned to Janet…"You just don't get it," he said.

Influencing people is based on a few simple ideas:

- That you cannot simply broadcast from your Hilltop and expect others to see your point of view
- Most people have their own perspectives, which are valid for them
- Most people resist being influenced if it means giving up their point of view
- People are more easily influenced if their needs, commitment, perspective, etc., are included rather than excluded

46 THE WORKSHOP THAT NEVER WAS

The strategy was to create collaborative project execution.

We developed a partnering kick-off workshop process to set the right climate at the start of each project. It proved very successful and consequently very popular amongst the project teams, both with suppliers and customers.

I received a call from a frustrated project manager about running a workshop. His project was not going well, the senior leaders were not engaged, and the project was getting stuck.

After some deliberations, we decided to meet with the customer's project manager and at least discuss a potential agenda, even if the senior leaders were not sponsoring it. However, when the senior leaders heard that I would be meeting the project managers, it triggered something and they decided to invite themselves.

To be at the early morning meeting was a long drive and an overnight stay. After some short introductions, the senior leaders got talking, and they started discussing the project and the key issues. This direct dialogue had not happened before, so we let it run, and in a short time, many problems were solved, and they came to an agreement on how to proceed with a commitment to meet regularly.

Afterward, the Project Manager was embarrassed and apologetic. He felt bad he had pressurized me to make the long trip, and now, with the senior leader dialogue, the main reason for the workshop was gone. I had wasted my time.

I took a different view.

As Edgar Schein, the author of Process Consultation, tells us, a consultant is a helping relationship and follows some simple principles; these include...

- It is the client who owns the problem and the solution
- Always try to be helpful
- Everything you do is an intervention
- Go with the flow

Was my involvement an intervention? Had it helped solve the problem? Did they feel ownership of the solution? Absolutely. I felt, for now, my job was done.

Change interventions might not meet our preconceived ideas, but staying focused on the overall goal is important, not for us, but for the client and, ultimately, the change you seek to make.

47 OVER 30 YEARS OF LAUNCHING PROJECTS

"You know your project is in the spotlight when you come back to your desk to find a post-it saying the minister of transport called, please call him back" explained the project manager.

His project was not going well; there were many more challenges than anticipated. Unfortunately, this was not the kind of project away from the public eye; it was a new signalling system for one of the busiest lines into London. With the huge delays it was no surprise he received the minister's call.

Projects are not easy, they are much more likely to fall short than over shoot. A project is a uniquely human endeavor that creates change, which is the root of their difficulty.

Bent Flyvberg, in his best-selling book "How Big Things Get Done," draws out his lessons from studying more than 16,000 projects from 20-plus fields and in more than 136 countries. He concluded from the data that a minuscule 0.5% of projects nail cost, time, and budget.

Without oversimplifying the solution Bent talks about "Think slow, act fast" or take time to plan as it speeds up execution. Highlighting the heuristics or ways of thinking that help and those that trip you up. He also illustrates his conclusions by looking at real-life examples like contrasting the projects of the Sydney Opera House, 1400% over budget, and Tgenheim Bilbao, 3% under budget.

"Planning is an unnatural process; it is much more fun to do something, and the nicest thing about not planning is that failure comes as a complete surprise rather than being preceded by a period of worry and depression."
Sir John Harvey Jones

Planning has a bad wrap. It's often considered a passive activity, like sitting and staring into space, abstract and bureaucratic. Time is short; let's get on with it. We feel more productive executing tasks than planning them.

My first company was an engineer-to-order business; these large, complex projects repeatedly fell short. The team I was part of researched the root causes and how they could be overcome. Part of the solution we developed was a project launch process to set up projects for success. The process unearthed assumptions and created a shared understanding and a focus on goals. A diverging process before converging.

We also observed that projects operate in an environment that is either supportive or obstructive. Leaders and Sponsors have the responsibility to provide a constructive environment. We had seen project managers left to solve the companies' problems to help their projects succeed; of course, this was not possible.

> *"Projects are often at the forefront of an organization's strategic plans and can therefore be seen as vital to the continued success of the organization"*

All of this is no less true for our HR projects. I have spent over 30 years launching projects and built a project launch pad for setting projects up for success, combining project management, change management, and design thinking.

Be a good sponsor, invest time into planning, you won't regret it.

48 BILLS FORM

"Minimize your therbligs until it becomes automatic; this doubles your effective lifetime and thereby gives time to enjoy butterflies, kittens and rainbows."
Frank Bunker Gilbreth & Lillian Moller Gilbreth

I stopped by Bill's cabin in the workshop. As I stood at the door, he barely looked up and mumbled, "Not today, Andy; I don't have time"

He was writing a long list of numbers, using a ruler to keep them straight. Not easily deterred, my curiosity kept me there. "What are you doing, Bill?"

"I am writing down part numbers and quantities to order the material from the store and get production back on track." Answered Bill

"That looks like tedious work." I observed.

"Tell me about it," said Bill. "my head is awash with part numbers; I even dream about them"

"There must be a better way." I replied, "You could produce a standard form, listing all the part numbers and then just put in the quantity. That would save a ton of time."

He finally looked up at me, sending daggers with his eyes. "I just have this blank form which I hardly have time to fill it out, let alone create a new one."

"Well, I think a few minutes to write down a standard list of part numbers would be a good investment of time."

"Clear off, I don't need your bright ideas." Bill was not happy; I was not impressed.

"Well, I'll leave you to your nonvalue-adding work then," I said pointedly, and off I went; I had a feeling we wouldn't be buying Christmas cards for each other.

A few weeks later, I passed by his workshop; he saw me and started walking my way. I was unsure what would happen; was this his chance to chastise me for my last visit?

"I'm glad I caught you," said Bill. I braced myself for what would come next.

"I didn't like your bright idea last time you were here" said Bill, he paused, "but I thought about it and you were right. I took home some paper and drew up a new form with part numbers at my dining room table one Sunday afternoon. My wife was not best pleased as she was expecting us to do something together."

"You know what, Andy, you can't believe how much time it has saved, and when the pressure is on adding quantities is faster, less stressful, and I make fewer mistakes."

In the following months, many other supervisors copied Bill's form. What can we conclude from this?

- Watch out for waste, challenge what you do, and look to continuously improve
- It's easy to get stuck in vicious circles, trapped by inefficiency
- Sometimes, you need an extra push and investment of time to break out, but you'll get the payback later

49 THE GREEN REPORT

I was unlucky.

In a meeting, my boss had agreed that I would split up and distribute the productivity reports each week.

Nicknamed the "green report". It was a huge block of computer print-outs on green paper (no surprise). Once split up, I needed to then send them through the post to a list of senior managers.

It was my first job, I was junior, so this is the kind of task you get. I got on with it and it became part of my weekly routine. I had learnt about continuous improvement and applied this to becoming more and more efficient in splitting up and distributing the reports.

Returning from my summer holiday, the green reports were waiting for me on my desk; well, who else would do it? But I started to wonder; nobody had asked for them while I was gone. How important were they really?

I asked my boss if he minded if I checked with each manager whether they still wanted the reports. "Go ahead" he said. I hand-delivered the next set of reports to ask each recipient whether they still wished to receive them.

"No" said the first senior manager, "I just put them in the bin."

"Oh, you are the person sending them to me," said the next manager. "My secretary just files them; if you keep a copy, I don't need them"

Finally, the last manager told me, "My secretary makes copies and sends them to the manufacturing sites. You can stop sending them to me if they don't want them."

I got the names and followed up with each site. "No" came the answer.

When I reached the person at the last site, he laughed, "What's so funny? I said.

"I wondered where they came from; I am the one printing and sending them to you."

As nobody wanted the reports, he stopped sending them to me.

I kept one page of the report and put it up on the wall behind my desk as a reminder.

Taiichi Ohno, an engineer at Toyota and Father of Just-In-Time Manufacturing, identified the seven categories of waste. Ohno always started with eliminating waste, then reducing what was left. It's a question of focusing on what really adds value.

I am struck by all the excitement around AI-powered systems, digitalization, and automated transcriptions; we might well be too quickly thinking about automating before questioning the value and importance of what we do.

After all, we might well be perpetuating waste!

Whatever our function or role, is there a waste you should challenge?

50   GETTING LUNCH

Here in Zurich, I work in a very international environment; you can expect to hear almost any language at the coffee machine, although it's typically English. However, when you step out of the office you immediately find yourself in the local culture and language.

We usually buy lunch from a takeaway called "Not Guilty." It's set up like most: you place your order at the till, the order gets passed to a team that makes it up, puts it into a takeaway box, and finally, to a collection point where another person calls out the order number for you to collect.

As German is the local language, it can create confusion with the many international employees and overseas visitors waiting for their order but not recognising their number has been called out. The orders start stacking up, people start asking where their order is, and the collection gets mixed up, frustrating the customers and the staff and slowing the process.

I recently noticed that my order was always being called out in English. At first, I thought it was because I was a regular, but I noticed it wasn't only me. The more I observed, the more I realized the person had started to call out the order number in the right language for all the customers even though, as last in the process, they had no idea to whom the order belonged, let alone what language they spoke.

Mulling over the mystery, I realized I was holding the key to the puzzle in my hand. There on the receipt with my order number was a line "Auf Englisch Ausrufen" or "call out in English".

I realized the one person in the process who does know what language the customer speaks is the person who takes the order. To pass that knowledge on they added a function to the till where the assistant selects the language the order needs to be called out in.

A simple process change that adds to the smoothness of the service delivery, supporting a great customer experience. They thought about the experience from the perspective of the first-time customer.

Clever but simple.

Quite rightly, there is a trend towards Employee Experience; as we drive quality in HR, we need to have an outside-in or customer-centric mindset.

- Are your HR services designed around your organization or how the customer looks for the service?
- Services designed for people very familiar with the process or for the first timer?

Let's challenge ourselves so we can serve the business and if needed "call out in English".

51 LEADING AN HR TURNAROUND

She sat in my office crying; the pressure was intense, and my office was the calm in the eye of the storm. She was resilient but even she needed somewhere to unload. This intense pressure was coming from the goal of doubling the size of the business in three years. Hindsight would show this was never going to be possible. The HR Leader had suddenly left the business; I needed to jump in, and what I found was a mess. The team had unpicked itself; things had not looked good from the outside, but it was much worse on the inside. I knew the team; they were good people, smart and hard-working, but they were frustrated. We needed to turn the situation around.

I have lived through many turnarounds in my career; the lessons have embedded themselves into me. These are the ten lessons that I applied to turn the situation around…

1. Diagnosis - Talk to as many people as possible, listen to what they have to say, and quickly figure out what is frustrating people and what is most important

2. Immediately increase communication - Run an "All Hands" call and then provide a weekly update after that. It is about transparency, shared understanding, and alignment.

3. Provide firm ground - there is often lots of emotion, doubts, and lack of confidence; let them know what is not changing, and provide reassurance.

4. Contract with the leadership team - Bring clarity and focus, agree your priorities, and plan so everyone knows what is important, this and no more (but keep something in your back pocket).

5. Execute your plan and don't get diverted - there are plenty of people who will try and add something, learn the word "No". You need some stubbornness to stay on track.

6. Find and bring in short-term resources to solve specific issues - you don't always need to grow the team, just get over the hump.

7. Manage the emotion - give people space; it's OK to have lots of feelings, navigate the ups and downs, let them unload but not get stuck, and help them move past it.
8. Listen to your team, believe in them - like they really know what they are talking about, back them up, and be open to reverse coaching. You are jumping in; a lot is new, so keep learning.
9. Give people what they need so they can do their jobs - back them up and move resources around to align with your priorities.
10. Address unhelpful behaviors - help the team play nice together; there are plenty of enemies, and your colleagues should not be one of them. If needed, change people.

Postscript

We left the Quarterly Board Review and went to a local restaurant to decompress and reflect on what had happened. As we walked, the head of the business turned to me and said, "Andy, I am amazed; you got a lot done in a very short period; you have completely turned HR around."

I smiled. "Well of course it wasn't me" I replied, "it was the team".

Actually, this was not entirely true. They were the same team members, smart and experienced, but their potential had been frustrated by the previous leader. They were ambitious; I had just done a better job providing direction and getting out of the way.

Good turnarounds follow a similar set of principles: bring direction, clarity, and empowerment. But we are not all designed to lead turnarounds. You don't just need a robust approach but you also need the ability to let stress situations calm you.

Be the calm in the eye of the storm.

52 DEDICATED FOLLOWER OF FASHION

They seek him here
They seek him there
His clothes are loud
But never square
It will make or break him, so he's got to buy the best
'Cause he's a dedicated follower of fashion

The song "Dedicated Follower of Fashion" was written by Ray Davies of the Kinks in 1966. The song was inspired by a fight he had with a fashion designer at a party. It's easy to wonder about the fickleness of fashion which has become increasingly based on the speed and turnover of trends.

When we start each year, it's when organizations go through priority setting. The research companies and consultancies provide surveys into what companies are prioritizing. The thought leaders are forecasting what they see as trends and innovations.

A friend asked me, "What do you think the big topics will be in the next 12 months?".

I wasn't trying to be clever or sarcastic, but something inside me reacted.

"Surely the priority is based on the business need rather than what everyone else is doing?" I responded. "We might have very different priorities to others."

In HR, have we become too fashion-minded?

Thinking back to the last few years we have seen the reinventing of performance management, launching skills management, throwing out competencies. Why did so many companies do this at the same time? What is the triggering event?

When scrolling through LinkedIn there is a temptation to look over everyone else's shoulder and then suffer an attack of FOMO. "Fear Of Missing Out". Beware the consultancies and thought leaders; they are in the business to provoke it. This makes many followers of the few innovators. The innovators knew why, but the followers may not. We reproduce what others are doing, and therefore, there is little uniqueness created. After some time, we are all looking and smelling similar.

So, when starting a new year, let's step back for a moment and consider…

…are our priorities really ours, or have we become Dedicated Followers of Fashion

WANT TO KNOW MORE

If you want to dive deeper into the topics covered in this book, below is a list of my suggested reading. There is also a companion diagnostic and workshop discussion guide that can be downloaded from my website.

www.thetalentculturecompany.com

Roy Calvert, Brian Durkin, Eugenio Grandi, and Kevin Martin, *I Just Love My Job! The "7P" Way to a Job You Love Based on Who You Are*, Nova Vista Publishing

Daryl Conner, *Managing at the Speed of Change: How Resilient Managers Succeed and Prosper Where Others Fail*, Villard Books

Stephen R. Covey, *The 7 Habits Of Highly Effective People*, Simon & Schuster

Bent Flyvbjerg, Dan Gardner, *How Big Things Get Done: The Surprising Factors Behind Every Successful Project, from Home Renovations to Space Exploration*, Macmillan

Edward, J. Hay, *Just-In-Time Breakthrough: Implementing the New Manufacturing Basics*, John Wiley & Sons Inc

Barry Johnson, *Polarity Management, 2nd Edition: Identifying and Managing Unsolvable Problems*, HRD Press

Spencer Johnson, *Who Moved My Cheese: An Amazing Way to Deal with Change in Your Work and in Your Life*, Vermilion

WANT TO KNOW MORE

Fred Kofmans, *Conscious Business: How to Build Value through Values*, Sounds True

George Kohlrieser, Susan Goldsworthy, Duncan Coombe, *Care to Dare: Unleashing Astonishing Potential Through Secure Base Leadership*, Jossey-Bass

John P. Kotter, *Leading Change*, Harvard Business Review Press

Ed Michaels, Helen Handfield-Jones, Beth Axelrod, *The War for Talent*, Harvard Business Review Press

Barry Oshry, *Seeing Systems: Unlocking the Mysteries of Organizational Life*, Berrett-Koehler Publishers

Megan Reitz, John Higgins, *Speak Up: Say What Needs to Be Said and Hear What Needs to Be Heard*, FT Publishing International

John Scully, John A. Byrne, *Odyssey: Pepsi to Apple: A Journey of Adventure, Ideas, and the Future*, Harpercollins

Edgar Schein, *Process Consultation Revisited: Building the Helping Relationship: Building the Helping Relationship*, Addison Wesley

Peter Senge, *The Fifth Discipline Fieldbook: Strategies for Building a Learning Organization*, John Murray Business

Ian Stewart, Vann Joines, *TA Today*, Lifespace Publishing

ABOUT THE AUTHOR

Andy Wild is the former Head of Talent, Culture and Change at ABB, a global leader in power and automation. He was the people workstream lead for establishing ABB's decentralized operating model, the ABB Way, which transformed the performance and culture of the ABB Group. Previously Head of HR for one of the global businesses that integrated ABB's acquisition of a large software business. His background comes from being a member of ABB's internal change consulting team in the UK.

A truly global citizen, he has worked in more than 30 countries and lived in the UK and Dubai, and is now a resident in Zurich, Switzerland, with his wife and daughter.

Andy now splits his time between writing and running his consultancy, the Talent Culture Company.

His motto.

British ingenuity, Swiss precision.

www.ingramcontent.com/pod-product-compliance
Lightning Source LLC
Chambersburg PA
CBHW072100110526
44590CB00018B/3251